FRIENDSHIP DEFINED

The 31-day remarkable journey to becoming a better friend

by Leilani Wood and Nicole Strickland

Friendship Defined

Published in Winston, Georgia, by Know Know Books®

WWW.KNOWKNOWBOOKS.COM

Cover Art by: Annalee Neeley of Black Swan Creatives

ISBN: 978-0-9824382-1-3

Library of Congress Control Number: 2021905965

Dedication

To our two kids who brought us together,
Kinsey and Charlie;

&

our three kids who witnessed our friendship
grow - and gained Aunts in the process-
Joshua, Nicholas, and Noah.
May you all be blessed with a friendship like
ours!
To our husbands, Clinton and Jason, thank
you for not only your love and encouragement
but putting up with us on a day-to-day basis
while supporting our friendship as it grows
along the way.

Welcome friends,

we invite you to visit

www.knowknowbooks.com

for a free gift

and to join our community.

"May the God of hope fill you with all joy and peace as you trust in Him so that you may overflow with hope by the power of the Holy Spirit."
-Romans 15:13 NIV

Dear New Friends,

We are so glad you decided to pick up this book and jump on this journey to strengthen your friendship with us. As we invite you into our inner circle, we want to give you a couple of things to keep in mind. This little gem that you are holding is meant to be conversational (so ignore the grammar, because you know that's not how you talk to your gal pals) Think of it as a 31-day devotional journey for you and your best friends. So, set the book down, grab your phone, and call your best friends and invite them to join you on this journey. Books for everyone! And if you're a real go getter, go ahead and start up a small group - next Sunday at 2 work for you? Each chapter may not be how you do friendship and that's okay. Go into this prayerfully - let it plant a seed of hope, not grow jealousy. This book is meant to spark conversations - tear the chapters apart, discuss it, and let God work in you and your friends as you dive into these chapters.

So put this book down, order a couple of copies or if you are my little loner buddy reading this by yourself, grab a cup of coffee, get comfortable, and let's get started on this walk together!

Love your New Friends,
Leilani & Nicole

Chapters

One

Webster Could Never Define

"Two are better than one, because they have a good return for their labor: If either of them falls down, one can help the other up." – Ecclesiastes 4:9-10 (NIV)

Like any great friendship, you can assume our friendship has stood the test of time. Currently, we've been BFF's for eighteen years. Wow! eighteen years! In most cases, if you've raised anything for eighteen years you know that by now it's graduating and off to college so you could pretty much say we are now working on our degree in friendship.

Together, we have been through a lot. We've had many ups and downs over the years. I mean, honestly, who hasn't made it eighteen years and not been through a lot? Our friendship is very important to us. We always keep God at the center of our friendship. But wait y'all- my God's got the whole world in his hands - he's not just in the center.

Being friends for eighteen years isn't easy peasy lemon squeezy. It requires a little work and effort.

It's always best to start at the beginning, so let's define friendship.

Mirriam Webster defines a friend as:

"1a: one attached to another by affection or esteem
Example: She's my best friend.
1b: acquaintance
2a: one that is not hostile, (_Is he a friend or an enemy?_)
2b: one that is of the same nation, party, or group
showbiz friends
3: one that favors or promotes something (such as a charity)
4: a favored companion"

The Urban Dictionary defines friends as:

"A person who would never intentionally hurt you, lie to you, deceive you, manipulate you, abuse you and who takes great care to be kind to you, honest with you, dependable and loyal. Someone who you trust without question because they have never given you any reason not to trust them. Someone you enjoy being around and look forward to seeing. Someone who would sacrifice themselves for you."

And this is just one of the many passages about friendship from the Bible:

"Two are better than one, because they have a good return for their labor: If either of them falls down, one can help the other up. But pity anyone who falls and has no one to help them up. Also, if two lie down together, they will keep warm. But how can one keep warm alone? Though one may be overpowered, two can defend themselves. A cord of three strands is not quickly broken." -Ecclesiastes 4:9-12 (NIV)

And *we* define friendship as:

Fun we have together (Myrtle Beach times two, road trips, celebrations, retreats, late night phone calls, talking extremely Southern)

Relaxing times (Lazy River, sitting on the beach, just talking, reading in random places)

Interesting moments (wrong way on the road, hospital visits, getting locked out of our hotel room, scaling sidewalks in superhero attire, and hurricanes)

Encouraging one another (you're the best BFF, quote cards, you were made for this, happy mail, little-yet meaningful- gifts)

Never-ending friendship, (Always and forever, as long as I'm living my BFF you'll be.)

Days, times, and memories we will never forget (Too many to list)

Thoughts to Think on:

- ❖ How do YOU define friendship?

- ❖ How do your friends define friendship?

- ❖ Are your definitions similar?

Act on It:

- ❖ Fill out the Friendship Acrostic with your best friend(s) using fun and memorable times from your own friendship.

Fun we have together

_____

_____

Relaxing times

_____

_____

Interesting moments

_____

_____

Encouraging one another

_____

_____

Never-ending friendship

_____

_____

Days and times we will never forget

_____

_____

"I typed a simple message, "Is Anyone out There?," virtually sending my SOS into the internet asking for help out of this darkness and back into the light."

Two

Is Anyone out There?

"You have turned on my light! The Lord my God has made my darkness turn to light." - Psalm 18:28 (TLB)

Leilani's story: The beginning of our story is kind of sad to share, and it involves some pretty personal information that I don't share with everybody, so consider yourself privileged.

I was at what felt like the worst of my worst. My life was hard and I had nobody to talk to about it. Don't get me wrong, there were people in my life, but sometimes you just don't feel like sharing things that are going on around you with them. It seemed like this weight was too heavy to put on anyone else's shoulders. Seriously, y'all, if something feels like it's so heavy that you're drowning, how could you possibly put that on somebody?

There's a lot that goes into this story, but I guess I'll just start with this big whopper: I placed my sweet baby daughter for adoption and I found myself in a pit of deep despair. The light didn't shine anymore; everything around me felt dark. I felt completely and utterly alone.

My last-ditch effort to save myself after days of crying and getting out of bed just in time to go get my son from preschool came in the form of a chat forum.

Depression had peaked to its height and I had never been depressed before- so this was very new to me. This pit of blackness seemed all-encompassing. So, here I was in the middle of the night in the worst pain of my life. I thought somebody has to know how I feel, there's gotta be somebody I can talk to, somebody I can lean on. I had met with my Pastor who had tried to help, but how could he guide me out of this dark forest if he had never been in these woods before? So, there I was still feeling alone in the middle of the night in front of my computer. I got on a search engine (and, no, I couldn't use Google; it wasn't a thing back then.) I entered a single word, adoption, and when I did an adoption forum appeared. I typed a simple message "Is Anyone out There?," virtually sending my SOS into the internet asking for help out of this darkness and back into the light.

Nicole's memories: Turns out at the same time Leilani was struggling, I too, was at what I felt like an all-time low in my life. I was sure I had hit rock bottom. Here I was, in my second unplanned pregnancy due to a failed birth control shot. (Meet the 0.01 percent. I checked with the record people and, no, there's no trophy for this one.) I was in no position to take care of a newborn baby, so I felt led by the Lord to make an adoption plan. Although placing my baby boy for adoption felt right in my heart, inside my mind was a different story. I quickly sunk into a deep depression and felt like no one understood the tug of war going on between what was right and true in this world around me versus what my heart and soul wanted it to be. I was left wondering, "could there be someone who understood the turmoil going on in my heart?"

Sleepless, and feeling utterly alone one night, I turned on my computer. As the bright light shone through my room, I pulled up a random search engine and began typing in adoption-related words. I wasn't even sure what I was looking for, when I found the term "birthmom" which ended up being the word I would now be forever called in relation to the son I placed for adoption. And then, finally, just as I was about to give up, I stumbled upon a recent, "Is Anyone out There?" post written by another birthmother. As I read her words and felt her SOS calling, I instantly realized I felt a little less alone. I quickly messaged her and eagerly waited for her reply.

Our completely dark worlds had been given a glimmer of hope. Now, over eighteen years later, neither of us realized what would come from that one post. And, here we are today; we have built an incredible friendship and sisterly bond. It has been quite the journey. We invite you to join us and learn what we think makes a strong friendship.

Remember, this book wasn't intended to be read in one sitting. We hope that you'll take it prayerfully day by day and read it with your BFF or bestie or even your small women's group and build stronger and better God-centered, lifelong friendships. We hope that you'll invite us to be your new besties by the time you finish this book.

Thoughts to Think on:

- ❖ What is a dark time in your life in which you really needed a friend?

- ❖ What friend was there for you?

- ❖ How were you a light to a friend during a dark time in her life?

"She's the
Ruth
to my
Naomi."

Three
Even If You're Slightly Cracked

"A friend loves at all times, and a brother is born for adversity." - Proverbs 17:17 (KJV)

One of Leilani's and my favorite friendship quotes is: "A true friend is one who thinks you are a good egg even though you are slightly cracked." She loves me when everything goes right, and she loves me when everything goes wrong- and even when my slightly cracked side is showing.

A friend loves you during your highs, and she better celebrates those highs with you. Heels and lipstick, watch out city, here we come! When I got married, Leilani was right by my side, well, metaphorically speaking, that is. We don't live in the same state, so through many, many phone calls, instant messages, and emails she helped me choose bridesmaids dresses, music for the ceremony, and plan my wedding. Thank goodness for technology, but Lord knows I could have used Pinterest back then. Girls, I had to take it old school with a pen, paper, and magazines. Leilani got there early to help me get those last-minute things prepared and to be sure my nerves were still in check. She stayed up with me into the wee hours of the morning laughing as we tied ribbons on programs, dotted every "i" and crossed every "t." And we may or may not have consumed more wedding candy favors than two girls should have consumed in one evening. She stood beside me as my hubby-to-be and I said our "I do's." Leilani celebrated that beautiful moment with me and loved me through what some may call bridal meltdowns and all that weddings are cracked up to be.

While I pray you have had many friends who have celebrated the high moments of life with you, the mark of a true best friend is one who is not only there through the highs but is there through the lows, loving you through those as well. I know I can turn to Leilani and often have in my darkest and weakest hours. My sweet, warrior son, Noah, is often described as a handful, and- while he is- I am quick to remind people that he is also a heartful. At times, he can be the sweetest, most caring, gentle spirit making sure the world around him has a blanket. While he is non-verbal and only communicates with limited sign language, he has a jovial spirit and is often trying to make others laugh and tease them. And while we cherish and treasure his good moments, not all are good; when he is in a mood, well, steer clear. Noah, who suffers from Autism, Cerebral Palsy, Epilepsy, ADD, and Scoliosis, sometimes has violent meltdowns. I hope you aren't familiar with what an Autistic meltdown looks like - so I'm gonna tell you. They are not pretty. Picture a teenage, special- needs boy upset about something, but he can't tell you what. He yells, his arms flail, he throws things, and hits anyone within reach. The only way to really stop these meltdowns is to hold him down (therapists teach you a special hold so neither of you gets hurt) and wait it out.

By the time these meltdowns are over, I'm often left feeling defeated, exhausted, and questioning whether or not I'm a good Momma and wondering if I did it all right. You see, as I said before, Noah's non-verbal, so I don't get the same reassurances other parents may get. I know the meltdowns are a part of Autism but sometimes it is really, really hard to not take them personally. Leilani is right there, a text or phone call away, lovingly walking through those adverse moments reminding me that I am indeed a good mother and that I am doing the best I can. I feel like a spiritually deflated balloon and she fills me up with- what at my best guess is- laughing gas and by the end of all this, we're usually on the floor rolling in laughter. I can truly say laughter is the best medicine.

While I'm spilling the beans on a little dirt, I'm ashamedly going to admit to what some might call being selfie-obsessed. It may be a slight character flaw or crack in my shell, you might say. Whenever Leilani and I are together, she lovingly endures me snapping 29 selfies in a row! I need 29 to get one decent one because of all the faces she is making at me. I mean, come on folks! Well, I can attest it's not easy. However, she recently admitted to me that while it is slightly annoying at the moment, one day when we are old and gray, she is going to treasure those photos and be glad I was always making us slow down just enough to take the time to capture that moment. Albeit, a small flaw, it's still a flaw and she's promised she loves me for it. A true friend loves your flaws too. In fact, your flaws are probably one of the things she secretly loves most about you because they make you, YOU!

You may have been wondering how I know Leilani loves me. Well, aside from the fact that she walked through Bridezilla, Mommy meltdowns, and selfies, she tells me and she does little things to express it. During every single phone call, text, email, etc., she makes me feel better. She is complementary but not in a fake kind of way; she genuinely means it. She builds me up and reminds me of my strength, but she also warns me to remember my limitations as well. She seems to just sense when I need a little pick-me-up the most, a little air for my balloon- you might say, and next thing I know, there's a card in my mailbox that is often handmade. Her gifts are always so well thought out and meaningful.

Friendship isn't one BIG thing, it's a million little things and wrapped in love.

Thoughts to Think on:

- ❖ What highs have you and your best friend celebrated together?

- ❖ How has your best friend loved you through adversity?

- ❖ What are some of the little things your friend does to let you know that she loves you?

- ❖ What are some of the little things you do to let your friends know you love them?

Act on It:

- ❖ Do a little something for your BFF to show her a little extra love.

Four

Who's That Girl?

"Whoever walks with the wise becomes wise, but the companion of fools will suffer harm." -Proverbs 13:20 (ESV)

There was a popular TV show that started back in the early 2000s. In fact, it might still be on the air now. The show had two best friends as the main characters. These characters referred to each other as "my person." The internet has now created a meme for this, and you may have seen it floating on the web, but we adopted this phrase in our friendship WAY before the meme of the 21st century.

So, maybe you are asking yourself what exactly do we mean by "my person?" For us, she is the one who has stuck by your side through thick and thin. She is your ride-or-die girl, who more often than not was there before husbands and children came along.

To try and explain this out, hopefully, this will give you a picture of what "my person" is.

My person is...

- The person who I call when I'm having the worst day, and when I hang up the phone, I forgotten why I was angry or sad in the first place.
- The person who shares my love for Christ and His word.
- The person who mails me silly things just to see me laugh.
- The person who will call my husband after I hang up the phone to say "Keep an eye on her. I don't think she's OK."
- The person I can talk to for hours about nothing and it only feels like 5 minutes, kind of like living out an episode of *Seinfeld* or *Friends*.
- The person who can complete my sentences (or edit my writing) because she truly knows my heart and is sure she knew what I meant to say.
- The person who I can just sit in silence with because, sometimes, words aren't needed. Just knowing they are with you can be enough.

- The person who will say, "Yes, your butt does look big in those jeans" and "No, don't just charge it."
- The person I can carry on an entire conversation with using movie quotes and song lyrics all while talking in a thick, fake Southern accent.
- The person who secretly tells my husband what I really want for my birthday.

So, we hope this paints a better picture of who my person and best friend is- the one I dreamed of, hoped for, and prayed for my entire life. Maybe we weren't playing on the playground in grade school as BFF's, but we have certainly made up for that. This friendship was definitely worth the wait. She is the Daisy to my Minnie. She is the Ethel to my Lucy. She is the Rachel to my Monica. She is the Ruth to my Naomi.

Thoughts to Think on:

- ❖ What is your definition of "my person?"

- ❖ What has she done for you to let you know that she is your person?

- ❖ What have you done for her to let her know you are her person?

Five

Are You My Facebook Friend?

"Greater love has no one than this, that someone lay down his life for his friends. You are my friends if you do what I command you. No longer do I call you servants, for the servant does not know what his master is doing; but I have called you friends, for all that I have heard from my Father I have made known to you." – John 15:13-15 (ESV)

In today's world, the word friend is used extremely loosely. Oftentimes, people confuse the words "friend" and "acquaintance." Ask a 10-year-old child who was just handed a happy meal at his favorite restaurant who his newest friend is? You better believe it's that smiling face behind the counter and if that same friendly employee gives that same kid ice cream, you better hold on tight, because he might just leave your good home for theirs. Now get one of those all-knowing teenagers to answer a simple question about their so-called "best friends" and most could not even tell you their friends' last name, their parents' name or even where they live and you'll hear the sound of crickets as typically they don't have any worthwhile answers. Then there is Facebook and other types of social media, people have hundreds of so-called friends but how much do they really know about these "friends?" Are they really there for you? I mean just try missing 30 days on social media and you're nearly forgotten. Suddenly the all-consuming friendship you once thought you had has been changed over to the next person who manages to comment, like, and shares the post the most. Sadly, this is the same case for some family members as well, but I'll hop off that soapbox before I climb too high and I fall and hit my head.

In my heart, and even in the Bible, a friend is a cherished person- someone who you know all too well and who knows you the same. So many people often say, "a friend accepts me as I am-" well, I call bull! While she does do that, a true friend loves and accepts you as you are but at the same time, she loves you so much that she encourages and gently pushes you to grow, change, and become a better person than you are today. The person at the checkout counter in your favorite store- you know the one that you say hello to and she asks about the family every single week, accepts you as you are, but friends, I hate to burst your bubble, she is not your friend. She is an acquaintance. Now don't get me wrong, this would be a very nice acquaintance that could grow to a friendship. But ladies, it's time we redefine the word friend. I know of a couple that renews their vows every five years; they do this because in those five years they have grown and changed a lot and really into new people. This is their commitment to each other that even though that growth has made them into completely new people they're committed to each other. We were not put here on this Earth to stay put; things that stay put too long die. Even when we accept Christ, we are completely transformed. Iron sharpens iron and that means there might be a little friction- and that's okay.

It's also important to note the difference between a friend and someone you share an interest with. It's great to have a long list of people you meet up with or visit on occasion for, maybe, a basket weaving 101 class, but really stop and think, "How close are you with those people?" If something happens to you, will that friend be at the hospital holding your hand? Is she who you call when you accomplish a goal and not just the "yay, I finished my first 8 layers, triple hook back diamond basket, want to see?" kind of call either. I mean, will she cheer you on in your goals and praise your accomplishments, or does she just tend to brag about her own accomplishments? A true best friend cares about and loves you, she truly knows you, cheers you on, will drop everything for you, and so much more. She knows your heart, dreams, goals, desires, fears, last name, parents' names, and where you live. And, the same knowledge goes for you too.

Thoughts to Think on:

- ❖ Think about who your true closest friends are.

- ❖ How much do they know about you, the real you, not just the trivial stuff? And vice versa?

- ❖ Are they willing to tell you if you are wrong?

Six

The Sister God Let Me Choose

"Friends can destroy one another, but a loving friend can stick closer than family." - Proverbs 18:24 (God's Word)

So, raise your hand if you have a sibling. Since you can't see us, we guess we should tell you both of us would have our hands raised right now because we have 9 siblings between the two of us. While we share things in common with our siblings, like DNA, parents, dimples on the nose, the need for glasses, and funny childhood stories, we obviously did not get to choose them to be our siblings. If you grew up in the "cross-stitch everything era" as we did, you probably saw a framed cross-stitched sign in a random house like your Aunt Wendy Ann's that read, "You can't choose your family, but you can choose your friends." As a kid I wondered, did she really like us or was she just trying to tell us something? Can we say subtle hints? We do both have to agree that this quote does have some merit because what we've learned by the time we reached adulthood was that we too wanted to choose those friends who

33

weren't just in this for a season but wanted a sister, who was in it for the long haul and maybe even a like-minded Christian.

Speaking of siblings, have you ever been on one of those family road trips as a child? We both have. Those are where we were taught to keep our hands and feet on our side of the car, ultimately teaching us to respect another person's boundaries and to this day, we both have not-so-fond memories of our brothers' stinky feet trying to creep over to our side of the car. We were also taught forgiveness and that when we have arguments with our siblings, we had to talk and work through them and then there was the hug. We're not too sure about your parents,, but we know of some parents who made their children get in the same oversized shirt and hug it out to accomplish this ridiculous goal. (Just try using this in corporate America today. Something tells us it wouldn't work.)

Those kids that were hugging in the shirt; they're your family. They're your relatives. It's a done deal. You don't get to vote on what nasty kid is in the shirt with you. But friendships -

well, they are different. Let's be real, the right friend is going to help you jump out of the car to get away from those stinky feet. And if y'all are stuffed in a shirt together, well that's just a party waiting to happen. While you might not have had that best friend as a child, life happens and God sends them when you need them the most.

The beauty in choosing your friends is that they get to know you for who you are in the moment you met them and who you are becoming, while your family knows and loves you for who you have always been. A friend has a way of helping you look to your future, while your family's roots are in your past.

But since best friends are the family you choose; you have to work to cultivate and build those relationships as well. By now, you are hopefully older and wiser when you are choosing your BFF. You don't just pick someone and become their BFF overnight; last time I checked kidnapping is still illegal. Even if it's an adult. Friendships take planned visits, scheduled phone calls, BFF date nights, etc.

For example, one of the things that we have done for years to stay close and connected in our own friendship is to have virtual tea time. Yep! You read that right- virtual tea time. Since we don't live in the same state, we would set the date, plan the theme, and pick the time each week to have tea together over the phone using the exact same tea set across two states. Because get-togethers keep you together.

Friendships take a conscious effort on all parts and if one is giving or taking more than the other for an extended period of time, it's likely to burn one of you out. Because unlike the kid you had to hug for an hour in Dad's shirt or the stinky feet sitting next to you on a never-ending road trip, you don't have a shared last name to fall back on. So, burnout can quickly lead to walking out.

Thoughts to Think on:

- ❖ What are the little things you have done in your friendship to keep you close together?

- ❖ Can you think of a time when your friend felt closer than family?

- ❖ What's something you can do to prevent burnout in your friendships?

"I want you to know that a Godly friend will not only accept you, but she will connect and love your "family" as well."

Seven

Ain't Nobody Gonna Rain on This Parade

"A cheerful heart is good medicine, but a broken spirit saps a person's strength." - Proverbs 17:22 (NLT)

There have been times Nicole and I have laughed so hard our sides physically ached from laughter and tears streamed down our faces. I think we have even laughed so hard that a drink or two has come out of the wrong hole on our faces! I don't want to even try and imagine a world without laughter and most especially without laughing with my best friend.

They say that laughter really is the best medicine, and I truly can attest to that one. Laughter often makes us forget our circumstances and trials and transports us to a happier time and place. I would much rather lose ten pounds laughing till my side aches instead of realizing that my spoon just tapped the bottom of my empty third container of Chunky Monkey ice cream because I was feeling down and depressed.

I'll never forget one of the saddest days of mine and my BFF's friendship. A young family member of her husband's had passed away. You're probably wondering where the laughter is in this one, aren't you? And while it is an odd place to giggle, this is one of my favorite memories of laughter in our friendship because I feel like God lifted our spirits while our hearts were so heavy. God gave us the best medicine we could have needed at that moment; He gave us each other and a healthy dose of laughter.

While waiting for the funeral to begin, we laughed at some of the smallest, silliest things. We sat side by side at the church consoling each other. Everyone probably thought, "Aw, look at them lifting each other up while holding back their tears." Oddly enough, and luckily for us, holding in laughter and holding back tears look a lot alike. But what those watching us didn't know is that we were whispering in each other's ears, "Don't you dare let that laugh out, girl!" All the while, little snorts were trying to escape.

Now, I know what you are probably thinking. How rude! You were at a funeral for Pete's sake. Show some respect. Well, yes, you may have a point there, we were but, when you write the word funeral, you have to begin with "F-U-N," right? We were not in denial sitting in

shock at a funeral, yet we were paying our
respects and biding time by laughing at
memories. We were healing with laughter and
joy for the life lived not the life lost. We were
being quiet and discreet and not causing a
scene. At that moment, I wanted to build my
friend's strength through laughter. I could have
joined in and painted what was already a sad
and dreary day with more sadness, and while
there were some true tears shed, God allowed
me to add a rainbow to an otherwise cloudy and
gloomy day.

Thoughts to Think on:

❖ Do my best friend and I laugh enough?

❖ What can we do to laugh more?

Act on It:

❖ Find a funny picture, quote, meme, or
joke and share a little laughter with your
BFF when she is feeling down.

"The words comforted me like a warm cup of hot chocolate on a cold, snowy day."

Eight

Big Girls Do Cry

"Weeping may endure for a night but JOY comes in the morning." – Psalm 30:5 (KJV)

Years ago, I desperately wanted to have another baby and after many months of trying, my husband and I finally saw those exciting two little lines pop up and we were pregnant. It felt surreal - a dream come true. I was so excited to be pregnant this go-round. You see, my previous pregnancies were unexpected and unplanned. Don't get me wrong, I love both of my boys but this pregnancy was different. When I was pregnant before, instead of being congratulated, people would say, "Oh no, what are you going to do?" There was the look of judgment and shame - you know the one I'm talking about. But this time, this pregnancy, THIS baby - it would be different. I was showered with congratulations and excitement as soon as I told someone - anyone- I was pregnant. The joy on their faces showed up. As you might have guessed by now, Leilani was the first person I shared the news with outside of my husband. Her excitement matched my own so much that I began to wonder whose news it was anyway. She cried happy tears with me and shouted with joy.

Sadly what we thought would be a long-lasting life with our baby did not last long, for our precious baby and our joyful excitement would suddenly end as she met heaven's gate before she had a chance to meet our arms. I was heartbroken and my whole body ached for the loss of our sweet baby. My husband and I decided it was important to us to have some sort of memorial service for our precious baby girl who -although, she hadn't taken an earthly breath yet- was very real to us. She was every bit our daughter and needed to be memorialized. We reached out to some friends and family to join us at a nearby lake for this memorial where we could pray and lean on each other over this loss.

Leilani had a lot going on at that time, and I knew coming to me would have meant she would be driving many hours each way with her 8-month-old baby, my namesake, Nicholas, but like any good and able-bodied friend she somehow, not too sure what she did to make it happen, nor would she have told me, but she made it work. She even showed up early to help with the little details of the memorial service. She knew that after today those would be all that I had left of my sweet baby girl.

During the memorial service, she was a gentle presence for me, holding my hand, giving me space, shedding tears with me, and saying the most beautiful, precious prayer over the balloons as we watched them float away like a vapor, a beautiful vision- here today, and in the blink of an eye, gone. She could see the pain I was in, and most importantly, she felt that pain with me. She jumped in with both feet in one of life's deepest pains - the loss of a pregnancy.

And while I believe all of that alone is what a friend does in a time of crisis, what happened next will never, ever leave the tender walls of my heart. The days after losing our baby were a fog of trying to deal with the magnitude of the loss we had just experienced. Every day while my husband was at work and my nine-year-old son was at special needs day camp, I would close the curtains, hide in my room with a comfy blanket and blast Natalie Grant's song "Held" over and over and just sob my little heart out. The words comforted me like a warm cup of hot chocolate on a cold, snowy day. All I could think was that I was angry at God at that point, and I pulled inward a bit needing a little space to figure out how to move forward and navigate this pain. Leilani gave me that space and did not try to fix my pain but was there enough to let me grieve through it and know I wasn't alone.

In one of my vulnerable moments, I finally opened up and shared with Leilani about a song I was listening to. As I began to explain about the song and the lyrics, she began to cry too because at that moment she realized she had been listening to the same song, "Held." And when she listened to those lyrics, she would pray and cry for me. Even though she was many miles away, we were still connected through God.

God promises that through rough, grief-filled seasons in life, joy always comes in the morning. Leilani was one of my joys during that season. Turns out, I was not angry with God. I was angry with the circumstances I was in. I was angry with the cards I had been dealt. Looking back now, that is one of the times I felt the closest to God in my life because that is one of the times I too, was Held. Sweet friends, I pray that you feel Held in your times of grief too.

Thoughts to Think on:

❖ Is there a time in your life in which a friend cried with you and was there for you during a rough season?

Act on It:

❖ Take a moment and let your friend know how much it meant to you to have her support during that time.

"A friend is more than someone who's got your back – she's got your heart too."

Nine

She's Got My Back... and Heart

"Above all else guard your heart, for everything you do flows from it."
– Proverbs 4:23 (NIV)

Have you ever heard the saying "I've got your back?" Well, I have and I'm sorry, to say if you haven't you might have been living under a rock. Anyways, let me break this down for you. It simply means that if something happens, I'll stand up for you. You better believe I'm back here keeping watch. Let someone dare throw a punch and you duck, then I'm coming out swinging. I've even heard police officers or military while going into dangerous situations, shout out I've got your "6" which Urban Dictionary basically says means, "I've got your back."

In true friendship, it's more than just having your friend's back; it's about having her heart too. God's Word tells us to guard our hearts above all else. All of those little words together have big and powerful meaning and if you continue reading, it explains why - guarding your heart will determine the very course of your life. The heart is a powerful thing and will guide you more than your mind at times so we must be careful who we let in and near it.

Nicole has always had my heart! We have worked together for many years. They say don't do business with friends and while I do stand behind that, I would say we are an exception to the rule because we have been making it work for eighteen years as we have run a business together. In those years, it has required a lot of writing, proofing, and planning. I will admit, writing is not my best area. If you've ever been on the other side of a message from me, you'll know that's true. I always need an editor by my side just a little bit more than a spell check. I mean, girls, I'm serious - I'm one big run-on sentence. The problem with having someone else edit your work is if that person doesn't know you well and have your heart in mind, they can edit YOU right out of it. They can remove the most important parts of what you're trying to leave behind. But since Nicole knows me so well and we've been besties for so long, she's got my heart in mind. She can beautifully edit my writings so well that oftentimes, I'm left unknowing what she removed, added, or changed.

In our business life, we had to create a brochure with our personal story. In perfect Leilani fashion, I sent Nicole one big run-on sentence and what I got back was a beautifully laid out, four-paragraph letter of exactly what I was trying to say. Y'all, it got me so much I had to go back and look and see what I actually sent her. This girl sounded so much like me - it was a little bit scary.

I'm so thankful and blessed to have Nicole as my best friend. She's always got my back (my IGY6) - but she's got my heart too. And, clearly my writing.

Thoughts to Think on:

❖ How has not guarding my heart in a past friendship hurt me?

❖ How can I keep this from happening again?

❖ Do I have my best friend's heart?

❖ Does she have mine?

"I've got your "6"
IGY6

Ten

Playground Rules for Life

"Lord create in me a clean heart."
- Psalms 51:10 (TLB)

This is a hard one to write and I don't want to step on toes here. I'm sure most of the time it's all in good meaning when you want to be your friend's one and only person, but ladies, we are not in kindergarten anymore.

Picture this: your best friend lets the new girl in class push her on the swing. You see this and stomp your feet, pout out loud, and you believe you must not be friends anymore. Now, why can't you just go enjoy the big slide on your own and be happy? (Well, honestly, this is another deeper issue right here and out of my pay grade!) Wouldn't it be nice if you had gone and enjoyed the big slide? Then the story could have gone this way... There you are sliding happily and your best friend comes to find you exclaiming "Hey best bud! Come meet my new friend! She can really push us high on the swing. Come play! I can ask her if she'll push you too." Voila! Now look, you both have a new friend! Your friend did not think of you any less, it's just the new girl can push her higher on the swing. And now with that new friend, you both get pushed high on the swing.

Perspective is great. Don't you wish we all had that at 6 years old? It would have saved a lot of pouting and stomping. Sadly, we don't even have that in our 20's let alone our 30's. We feel like that one friend completes us and adding someone else might tear us apart. We don't need our friends to complete us and do everything with us to feel loved by them. You are an amazing person on your own merit, however, God created you to be relational. He did not say pick one friend solely and no more. I mean Jesus himself walked around with 12 others all with different talents, backgrounds, and abilities. I love that my very best friend Nicole has other wonderful friends. They bring so much joy to her life and can minister to her in multiple ways and often in ways I cannot. They are perpetually pushing the swing higher than me. I am not perfect by any means and I definitely don't know everything and ladies, guess what? I'm fine with that.

I am reminded of a time Nicole was going to change the type of food her family was going to eat in a more natural approach including cooking in new ways. This is not my area of expertise and because I love her I would much rather she obtain her goals and succeed in all areas and wouldn't stand in the way of her getting outside help so we can celebrate them later. That's when she enlisted another friend of hers for guidance and by doing so obtained her goals in this new area of life. If I found out she missed opportunities or ignored them because she was afraid that I would get my feelings hurt and stomp and pout or even feel left out over her talking to another friend and not me; I would be so greatly grieved. "Why?" you might ask. Because I love her and loving someone means wanting the best for them even if you're not the one to give it to them.

Sometimes you are the one to help your friends and other times you are the one cheering them on. So in the good words of Sherlock Holmes- "This is all elementary, my dear Watson, elementary."

Thoughts to Think on:

❖ Do I rely on one friend too much to fill my needs?

❖ Am I smothering our friendship?

❖ Do I have the wrong attitude when my friend mentions someone else she talks to?

❖ Would I go to my banker for plumbing advice?

Eleven
You Go Girl!

"Listen to good advice if you want to live well."
- Proverbs 15:31 (MSG)

Have you ever met one of those introverted and extroverted types? You may know the type; she may be outgoing and bubbly with people she knows pretty well but her shyness and the introverted side comes out when she is around a crowd. Well, that's me. If you ever left a party and hid in the closet or a bathroom just to have a minute to yourself then, you are probably one of us too.

So, a few years back, Leilani and I had to give a speech together. Leilani had the bright idea to do a monologue at the beginning of our speech acting out how we met. Wait a second, though, remember that little description I shared that described me as the introvert? Well, Leilani is the exact opposite.

Back to where we were, we knew if done correctly, it would be dramatic, impactful, and very meaningful. But I was terrified. A speech I thought I could fearfully manage because I could have note cards. But a monologue, I'd need to remember and just go with it. Reading from note cards would take away from the intensity of what we had planned.

Leilani knows me well enough to know that I'd be nervous but she instantaneously turned into my very own enthusiastic, personal cheerleader. Now don't get me wrong, she's not going to push me to do something I don't want to do, but she knew that I wanted to do the dramatic monologue but I was afraid. She coached me and gave me a pep talk giving me a play by play utilizing the skills she knew I had to accomplish our goal. She practiced with me, more than we probably actually needed to, but enough that I was comfortable. But let's be honest, as comfortable as an introvert can be.

And then, just before we were about to begin our presentation, she gave me one final pep talk that pushed me right through those pesky nerves. And you know what? Together, we rocked that monologue and I conquered that fear with her. It was like going on a roller coaster ride, where you are really scared for that first ride but the thrill is so exhilarating that you are ready to do it again. That's exactly how I felt about our monologue and speech - I was ready to go again.

It's easier to do things we are afraid of when we have our own personal cheerleader cheering us along. Be the type of friend who is a cheerleader. Encourage your BFF to conquer those nerves and fears that may be holding her back but more importantly, put those words into actions and grab the second mic and be her back up girl at karaoke night or strap on a parachute and jump out of the plane with her. Leilani picked up the mic that day and was more than just a backup girl. She was my parachute and lifeline. Now that's a mic drop, ladies!

Thoughts to Think on:

- ❖ What is something that you were afraid of that you were able to conquer because of your BFF cheering you on?

- ❖ What is something that your BFF currently wants to do but is afraid to do?

Act on It:

- ❖ Think of some ways that you cheer on your BFF in accomplishing something she is afraid to do.

Twelve

Connecting the Dots

"But Ruth replied, "Don't ask me to leave you and turn back. Wherever you go, I will go; wherever you live, I will live. Your people will be my people, and your God will be my God. [17] Wherever you die, I will die, and there I will be buried. May the LORD punish me severely if I allow anything but death to separate us!" - Ruth 1:16-17 (NLT)

So, question here: do you remember those connect the dot pages your teacher would give you if you finished your work early in those simple elementary school days? Well, I do. I was a very impatient child and a bit of a teacher's pet, so I usually rushed through my work so I had the pleasure of doing many connect the dot pages. I'd grab my favorite color marker, probably pink back then, and I'd connect the dots to see the beautiful picture emerge right before my eyes.

Friendship often reminds me of those connect the dot puzzles. You connect the dots between traits, hobbies, and maybe even favorite silly Christmas movies (ours may or may not be *Elf!*) or whatever else that you and a friend have in common and then your beautiful friendship emerges.

Those dots not only include the traits and things that you and your friend have in common but they also represent your family; the ones God gave you and the ones you have adopted along the way. I want you to know that a godly friend not only accepts you but she will connect and love your "family" as well.

I know God chose me to raise a child who as you have read before has special needs. Raising our sweet Noah who is unpredictable and wildly energetic at times, makes things a little interesting and chaotic at the same time. Instead of the typical parenting most parents can follow, my parenting style I'm sure often looks like I'm managing controlled chaos. I'm using that controlled word pretty loosely here. If you were to pull back my tattered and torn superhero cape (because let's face it, all Mommas are superheroes, am I right?!) you'd see my superhero name plastered across my cape reads "Chaos Manager."

Our Noah loves his routine and repetition. Let me draw attention to the words *his* routine here, not mine. And he'll tend to act out the only way he knows how. I recall one day, I sang "Itsy Bitsy Spider" 59 times. You think I'm exaggerating. And boy, do I wish I was. Truthfully, I'm probably exaggerating too lowly here.

Let's be real here. Although I know I am exactly where God intended me to be, there are times where raising a child with special needs is extremely difficult and just plain old physically and mentally exhausting. There are days where all I do is deal with meltdowns and listen to the same song on repeat (don't be fooled here, it's not one of my favorites) and by the end of the day, I have nothing left to give anyone. Sometimes it makes it difficult to have friends and I feel like I'm not a good friend.

God knows my heart on this and he blessed me with a very empathetic BFF. While Leilani can't specifically relate to what I'm going through with Noah at any given moment, she does an incredible job of putting herself in my place. She accepts the fact that although we may have planned to have a BFF phone date at 9 pm or maybe we were going to work on this book on a very specific inked in Tuesday night but because Noah is having a meltdown, a seizure, or maybe just a bad night, those plans might flip on a dime and before you know it I'm covering up those plans with a rescheduled sticker in my planner for the tenth time! Leilani has never once made me feel like a bad friend. In fact, she helps me find joy in the fact that I've been able to use that silly sticker so many times, and then she goes on to say, she even admires my patience with Noah. Here she is, always ready to connect the dots from my sadness to something I enjoy, my planner, making me laugh and temporarily forget why I was down in the first place.

I remember when we were trying to communicate better with Noah, it was suggested to us that we use ASL - that's American Sign Language. At that moment, Leilani decided to teach not only herself but her family ASL too so they could communicate with our little boy. Mind you, we live 4 hours apart, so it's not like our kids are together that often but, in her acceptance, and need to connect her boys to my boy, she taught them sign language and, more importantly she taught them acceptance and connection with others through her loving example.

Connecting the dots between your life and your bestie's life only makes your friendship thrive and grow stronger. Soon you will see a beautiful picture emerge in your friendship.

Thoughts to Think on:

- ❖ In what ways have you connected the dots between yourself and your BFF's family?

- ❖ What are some ways you can connect yourself to your BFF's family?

"It's easier to do things we are afraid of when we have our own personal cheerleader cheering us along."

Thirteen
Drop It Like It's Hot

"And don't forget to do good and to share with those in need. These are the sacrifices that please God."
- Hebrews 13:16 (NLT)

Alright, girls, I'm just going to get a little deep, a little raw, and a little real right here. I can clearly remember a time in my life where it felt like my world came crashing down around me. You see, I had been with and married to my high school sweetheart now for 12 years and my life seemed completely normal when I woke up on that particular St. Patrick's Day morning. I hurried about getting our 9-year-old son, Joshua, off to school with his leprechaun trap in tow and then I put our little guy Nicholas, who was 2 years old, in his high chair for breakfast. I then paused at the top of the stairs for a moment to give my husband a long hug and kissed him goodbye. Little did I know this would be the last time I would kiss him, the last time I held him, and the last time he felt like he was my husband.

Within a few short hours, I received a phone call that would change my life forever. I was let in on a secret that my husband was living another life and chose to leave us that day. At this moment, he felt like a stranger to me. So, here I was wondering how I was going to juggle my new circumstances. I was jobless because the very person I had worked with and for had just left. I was homeless because I found out the bills had not been paid and we were being evicted. And when I had the chance to look, the bank accounts were all overdrawn. And what I was left with was these two sweet little boys and the heart-wrenching reality that I now had to break the news to them that their Daddy was not coming back and this was no longer going to be our home.

I knew that I had to move in fast gear to tackle the list ahead of me in priority. First things first, get the kids to a fun location away from this craziness just in case Mommy begins to crumble at the weight of it all. They would not be here to witness it. My friend Karen's house was that retreat for them. She lovingly kept my boys never telling them of the circumstances unfolding.

Step two was to get all belongings moved to a new location quickly. My parents stepped in with a storage place that I could keep all of my stuff in for the interim while I figured out what to do. My friends Marty and Tracy rented a U-Haul for all of this to take place. After that long laborious night, they knew I would need a place to go. It wasn't an option they could offer long term but, honestly, what I needed that night and looking back separating that first horrible, very long night from my new normal is just what God knew I needed. He knew I needed long into the night counseling and a safe place to "feel all the feels" as they say- a place to get my head clear and try to make sense of my new upside-down world. Thankfully, Karen knew a few hours would not suffice and offered to keep the children overnight so that they could play and have one last night of normal while I wrapped up moving. This night was going to be hard but tomorrow was going to be even harder as I didn't know where we would end up. That is until number 3 (housing) was able to get checked off the list when my friend Gretchen (and Mommy to my nephew) showed up and opened her heart and home to us all. My nephew gladly shared a room so that me and mine could have his room. These things were being taken care of. God was showing up in ways that I never could have imagined.

So safe to say at this point in my life, I didn't know heads from tails, but it was coming along. I was frantically job hunting now and I didn't know much about my day-to-day life. But what I did know, thanks to every retail store between here and Egypt, was that Easter was fast approaching. Easter was always a big deal in our house. We'd always done up big beautiful baskets, elaborate egg hunts, and celebrated the beauty of new life and Christ's resurrection. Now I had to tell these two little angels that not only did Daddy leave, but there's no hope of an Easter Bunny in sight either. I know this may seem trivial and superficial and I know we live in a first-world country and there are children in other countries with far worse things to worry about tomorrow, but sweet friends, please understand these are my babies and what mattered to them mattered to me and this mattered to them. And while it mattered to them, it had fallen completely off my list, but praise God that it had not fallen off Nicole's list. While she was watching God deliver me out of so much of this with so many friends stepping in to help, she too was wondering how in the world she could step in and how God would use her and her husband.

So, while Nicole was tackling that, the next thing I had to tackle was those bank accounts. They were still in the red because I hadn't had the courage, let alone the money to fix the damage he had created yet. So, to go to the bank and explain what had happened with my husband and get this cleared up was not something I was ready to handle. I still hadn't come to grips with it myself so you can imagine I wasn't ready to pour out my heart and soul to a complete stranger and utter the words my husband left me. I have been with this man since I was 15.

While I was there trying to figure out which way was up, Nicole was in her own world devising a plan that I was totally unaware of. While I was trying to find heads from tails, she was trying to create the best Easter for my kids. So unbeknownst to me, the Friday before Easter, I had a surprise knock at the door and there was my best friend, Nicole, and her little family with all of Easter in tow. They had baskets filled with fun trinkets, their favorite candy, and even school supplies but most of all arms open with lots of love. When I asked Nicole if she wanted me to get the boys so she could give them the baskets, she said no, these aren't from me, they are from the Easter Bunny.

So, I wept at Nicole's sweet heart and the knowledge that the Lord used her to not only fill Easter baskets but to fill a hole in my heart that had been left just a few weeks prior feeling empty and alone. I was reminded that the Lord cares for us and he has people around us that he uses for his glory. It takes a special friend to be open to the knowledge that God is calling them to do far more through their actions and being the Hands of Christ. Instead of remembering the tragedy of the time, these boys remembered that Mommy's best friend, Aunt Nicole, showed up unannounced with the best school supplies and gifts that they could have asked for. She bought the boys the cool stuff, not the plain stuff Mom normally buys, but the cool, glow-in-the dark stuff. The world felt so dark and her actions brought light.

I also wept knowing this was a labor of love. I know money can be tight when you are already shopping for your own family. Time can be stretched thin on any holiday and travel can be nearly impossible when you have a special needs child of your own. But with love and armed with the knowledge that with God all things are possible, miracles can happen, and a broken heart can begin to mend through simple acts of love and kindness.

Thoughts to Think on:

- ❖ When have you dropped everything for a friend in need?

- ❖ When has a friend dropped everything for you? How did it make you feel?

"Sometimes, friendship is being a prayer warrior more than a prayer partner."

Fourteen

Livin' on a Prayer

" Therefore confess your sins to each other and pray for each other so that you may be healed. The prayer of a righteous person is powerful and effective."
- James 5:16 (NIV)

I hope by now that you are not only praying for your friends, but I hope that you have learned that you can pray with them too. Some of my fondest memories during my and Leilani's friendship involve times we have prayed with each other.

There have been several instances I can recall times in our friendship when I've had a major event coming that I was scared or nervous about. Leilani would know my schedule and always call me before the event so we could talk for a few minutes and then spend some time with the Lord together. I can vividly remember one instance where I was really, and I mean really, really, sick. (I know the editor and writer in me agree that I might not need all three reallys in the previous sentence but what you should know is that I was really sick.)

I honestly didn't have the energy to hold the phone and talk to her, but what I did know was hearing her words and her prayer would make me feel better, so I powered through and dialed those ten digits I knew by heart and laid the phone on my pillow and rested my head on the phone. I was right. I was comforted by her words and I had her prayer running through my mind as they placed the mask on my nose and I drifted off to sleep during surgery the next day.

Those prayers have grown even more necessary as our children have grown and our lives have become more hectic. But, with the business of our lives and children, there are times that we each want to pray with the other, but we just don't have the ability to drop everything and make a phone call. But, we can easily text one another a sweet note of encouragement or prayer.

And don't get me wrong, our prayers with one another don't always have to do with stressful moments or times of illness. I can remember praying with each other and praising God for blessing us right before each of our weddings, babies, jobs, and accomplishments.

I think it's important to remember to not only pray with one another during times of sadness but to praise God with one another during times of joy.

While I am comforted by knowing that I have a friend that prays for me, the moments we have prayed with one another are some of our treasured moments of friendship and those moments have made our friendship stronger.

Thoughts to Think on:

* ❖ Do you pray with your best friend?

* ❖ How can you pray with your best friend more?

Act on It:

* ❖ Set aside a time to pray with your BFF right now.

"Don't be ashamed
to set
limits and boundaries."

Fifteen

As the Clock Strikes

""At the right time, I, the Lord, will make it happen."
-Isaiah 60:22b (NLT)

As I sit here pondering to write this, I am often amazed at all that kings and queens and other world leaders accomplish in a mere 24 hours. How in the world do we fit it all in? Have you ever had a moment where you've had the best day and you want to call your best friend and share- or, maybe it was the worst day and you just need to vent. And this minute felt like just the perfect moment to call her and tell her everything that is going on in your world, only to be met with the polar opposite who doesn't sound like herself because you called when she was - pause - insert real-life here such as cleaning up poop for the sixth time, stubbing her toe, burning dinner, or trying to help with common core math.

I can safely say I've been on both sides of this coin. It's no secret that I'm a real person with a full calendar too. So, heads up, when you call a friend, be sure it's a good time for her to talk and don't, I repeat, don't get upset if it's not a good time for her. Instead, you can take this time to pray for your friend even if you don't know what's going on. Let's remember, they're real and living an entirely different life than you. And girls, don't forget our friend "modern technology-" texting or email are both viable options to help us busy friends juggle it all and stay in touch.

So, the next time your friend needs to let you go abruptly, then let them go without making them feel guilty or bad about it. Remember that they have a life happening on the other end of the phone. Nicole and I tend to have more of a phone relationship than an in-person relationship because we live in different states, so we have spent more time talking on the phone throughout the years than together face to face. Regardless, whether you are visiting one another or you are chatting on the phone, be open about how much time you have to give. I know it's hard because you never want to hurt your friend's feelings, but don't be afraid to let her know your agenda too. For instance, here's a couple of examples of how that conversation could go.

- Girl, I would love for you to stop by, but you'll need to head out by _____.

- Let's chat around ___, but I can only talk till___.

- Of course, I would love to visit you, but I'll need to leave by _____.

- Let's catch up around ___ PM. I have about _____ minutes free.

Don't be ashamed to set limits and boundaries. It's healthy. In the early years of mine and Nicole's friendship, we had weekly tea dates where we set aside time after our kids were in bed and our households were calm and quiet. We'd each make a cup of tea and talk on the phone. We even had matching teacups and looked forward to those scheduled times but we were also understanding and real when things popped up and we needed to reschedule or when life got hectic and we couldn't talk for a week or so at a time. The beauty of that was knowing, when life calmed down my best friend was there waiting for me with a teacup in hand.

Thoughts to Think on:

- ❖ How can you nicely let your BFF know when it is not a good time to chat?

- ❖ Are you respectful of your friend's time?

Sixteen

I Just Called to Say I Love You

"Kind words are like honey—
sweet to the soul and healthy for the body.
-Proverbs 16:24 (NLT)

Here's a little unknown fact: Leilani was the first non-significant other (well aside from my Momma, my Grand-momma, or some other relative) to say "I love you" when hanging up the phone. I honestly don't remember when she first said it because we've been friends for over 18 years, so I am sure it was eons ago by now. However, I do remember thinking that it was a sweet sentiment to end a phone call with and being slightly surprised that she said it. But now, almost no matter how short or hurried a convo may be, we rarely end a phone call without a quick, "Love you."

Girl, I know there are some people who don't believe in exchanging that sentiment every time they end a phone call; maybe they think it loses meaning each time you say it. And to each her own, but I assure you every time we hang up that phone, we've meant those three little words. If for some horrible reason that was my last ever phone call with Leilani, I'd want those words to be the last she heard from me and the last I heard from her.

I'm not saying that you need to tell your friend that you love her every single phone call just because we do. And I'm not saying it needs to be said at the end of a phone call. You do you, boo. But what I am saying is that we do need to tell our BFFs how much they mean to us occasionally. Let's be real here, not to be vain or anything, but sometimes it's just nice to hear that you are loved and how much you mean to someone.

A couple of years ago, I ended up in ICU via ambulance due to really high blood sugar. It was very scary and had my husband not called 911 when he did, I could have lost my life. I went home from the hospital feeling extremely grateful. I know we all often say life is short but that little come-to-Jesus health scare was eye-opening as to how short life really is, or can be, so now so more than ever, I really think it's important to take any opportunity you can to let others know how blessed you are to have them in your life. I hate to break it to you, but we aren't promised tomorrow, so we need to take those precious moments today. As Christians, godly friends, and just decent human beings we need to lift each other up, and as Leilani often says, "speak life" into each other. In a world filled with turmoil, grief, and sadness, we need to use kind, positive, and uplifting words from a place of love, respect, and encouragement any chance we are given.

Show your gratitude and love for your friend through your own words or try some of ours below:

"Thank you for being available today."
"I love it when you _____."
"Thank you for taking care of yourself."
"Thanks for doing _____ for me."

Or you can just sing a few lines of "I just called to say I love you" in your best Stevie Wonder impersonation.

Thoughts to Think on:

❖ When is the last time you told your best friend how much she means to you?

Act on It:

❖ Take a minute to let your BFF know just how much she means to you.

Seventeen

I Found Myself a Cheerleader

"Some people make cutting remarks, but the words of the wise bring healing."- Proverbs 12:18 (NLT)

Alright, girls, put your game face on. Sometimes all you need are your cheerleaders to get you motivated. A cheerleader knows what the score is, but they have an attitude and excitement that will push you forward. They don't pretend that the game is always in your favor. Sometimes there is more to the game than just the score. According to the scoreboard, we always win or lose but I believe we can always win if we learn something from the game. I think a cheerleader can see the potential the team has and can envision the win. They believe in a team so much that they stand on the sidelines and shout, yell, and rally for their team. Since cheerleaders aren't even touching the ball you could easily dismiss their importance, but they hold a high value to the team because they are constantly encouraging and pushing them to succeed.

Sometimes life just hits you right between the eyes like a ball to the face and knocks you on your butt and you don't want to get up. You just want to lay on the ground afraid you'll get hit again. My best friend and I both have a hundred examples of this exact event. I remember one instance in particular when I had been given sudden exciting news about a promotion I was being handpicked for. I just needed to do a few technicalities and in less than 10 days I would change the job I had for almost 10 years. It was so fast, yet adventurous and exciting. It was a dream come true.

Then, suddenly it was taken away just like that. I was in a little pit between sadness and "oh-my-goodness snap out of it." I still had a job and other people had many horrible things happening in their lives that were way worse than my little dream crashing. When I called my person, my best friend, my cheerleader in life, she was sad with me, but she didn't enable me to stay on the ground. She first let me know that it was ok to be upset and that I wasn't silly for being sad and that she would feel the same if her dream had been snatched away as mine had. She reminded me that I had it in me to get that job and that I was worthy of that promotion- but more than that, she was able to breathe new life back into my dreams. Never once did she dismiss the importance of what had just occurred. Somehow, she was able to turn this around and helped me see that this was just a steppingstone in a different direction on a brighter path. With her help and encouragement, I was able to brush the dust off myself and while I still had a bruise from the

89

fall, I also had a new vision and hope for the next quarter in this game called life.

Nicole never belittled the decision of the company not awarding me the promotion- that would not have helped heal my heart nor get me off the ground. Sure, it sounds like it would help to bash the other side, but it only adds weight to keep you on the ground. I've never enjoyed haggling with other teams anyway. We should be the best friend we can be by using our energy positively and wisely to encourage our team.

Thoughts to Think on:

- ❖ When is a time your BFF cheered you on?
- ❖ How did it make you feel?
- ❖ What can you do to cheer your friend on right now?

Eighteen
Mirror, Mirror

"Just as a body, though one, has many parts, but all its many parts form one body, so it is with Christ. For we were all baptized by one Spirit so as to form one body—whether Jews or Gentiles, slave or free—and we were all given the one Spirit to drink. Even so the body is not made up of one part but of many."
- 1 Corinthians 12:12-14 (NIV)

So, Nicole and I have often said had it not been for the major emotionally sad event in our lives that caused us to meet, we may not have ever been friends.

Typing that very sentence saddens me to the core for many reasons:

1. Are we that shallow?
2. Could I have a life without her?
3. Sadness was our initial bond and that just sounds, well, depressing.

But God is so good. When I think about my deepest conversations with the Lord, they too were from heartache and yet they are some of my favorite memories. "Why?" you might ask. Because those conversations were real and raw - not the covered up, polished version of me the world gets. They were the dark circles under the eyes, snotty-nosed, real-deal stuff. That's what our friendship is and what all deep friendships should be: REAL.

R- raw
E- emotional
A- authentic and covered in
L- love

With my hand-picked BFF, we can both be our real authentic selves. One of my worst qualities is (believe it or not) spelling and grammar. It's funny typing these very words because I know it's going to be in this book. But you can surefire believe that Nicole will have read and re-read and edited this before anyone else's eyes view it. Nicole doesn't make me feel bad for one or four (or more!) misspelled words, forgetting commas, or for all together leaving out punctuation. She's able to be real with me and edify me to be the best, polished version that I can be, you know, the one that you guys get. But, I believe she still loves the unpolished version with the dark circles under the eyes.

Do you want to know a juicy little secret about my best friend? It just so happens I have one or two. (Don't worry she's going to read and edit this, so I'm not sharing anything I haven't gotten the OK for.) One of her weaknesses is self-confidence, which boggles my mind. You see, she comes across as very confident, and not many people even realize that she second-guesses herself all the time, but I do because she can be completely real with me. This chick has published articles in magazines and books. She's had well-known television show producers calling her for advice on adoption. She has a successful blog and works with multiple nonprofit organizations, including her own, and she struggles with confidence? Are you kidding me, right now? I mean heck, I can run down to the local bookstore and read her words in a real book, and I'm not talking about this masterpiece you are holding in your hand right now. I'm talking about a book before this little gem came to existence.

But in all fairness, I understand that and all I know to do is give her reassuring words and remind her of how amazing she is to me and the rest of the world who can see past the fog stain over her own eyes. So, I put on my fighting gear and give Satan the one-two punch, so she has some confidence built back up. I remind her who she is so that when she looks in the mirror, she sees who God sees along with the rest of us.

Satan is a liar, folks. And being entrusted with a best friend means that you need to give Satan that one-two punch from time to time and help your friend remember who they are and not who the mirror says they are. It's our job as their friend to encourage them and build them up.

Thoughts to Think on:

- ❖ What lies does Satan try to tell you when you look in the mirror?

- ❖ Ask your BFF how she sees you. In what ways are your views different or similar?

Nineteen

525,600 Minutes

"Teach us to number our days, that we may gain a heart of wisdom." - Psalms 90:12 (NIV)

A popular song from the musical, *Rent,* has taught us exactly how many minutes there are in a year: 525,600 minutes. That seems like a huge number, right? But when you break it down and throw in other commitments and responsibilities such as your career, family, church, hobbies, health, etc. at the end of the day you may only have mere minutes left. As busy women, I know the last thing we want to do is add something else to our never-ending to-do list but trust me on this, new friends, making time for your friend benefits you in so many ways.

Leilani and I are both believers in the truth bomb that friendship is like any other relationship in your life and just as you put in the time and work with those relationships, you have to set aside time and work for your friendships as well. You can't expect to have a ride-or-die-type friendship with someone if you are not making time for them.

Spending time with your bestie strengthens and deepens your connection over time. I have pretty much been close to Leilani since about day 3 of meeting her but over time that connection has grown and deepened so much. Over eighteen years later after day 3, we really are like sisters. She knows me almost as well as I know myself.

Spending time with friends is also known to reduce stress. In such a busy and hectic world, we're all looking for ways to lighten the load of stress a little. Hanging out with your BFF or just talking to her for a bit can often reduce stress and make you feel lighter. And if you're lucky like me and have a hilarious, should-have-been-a-comedian BFF (seriously, she is THAT funny!) the laughter that ensues from talks or time together is medicine to soothe a weary soul.

Since we don't live in the same state, we have, at times, had to get pretty creative with how we spend time with one another. One of my fondest friendship memories has been our weekly (on the phone) tea nights. We had the same teapot and teacup and once a week, we'd each make tea, talk on the phone, and drink our tea together while catching up on what had been going on in each other's lives.

It honestly doesn't matter what you are doing with your bestie, but if you need some suggestions or new ideas to liven up your friendship, don't worry, we've got you.

- Pray together - Whether you are praying for each other, mutual friends, or just others in your lives, the BFFs who pray together, stay together.
- Road trips or vacays - Road trips are some of my favorite memories. Pack up some snacks, find some great 80s tunes, and hit the open road. Lots of laughter up ahead at mile marker 117.
- Celebrate your friendship anniversary - We refer to this day as our friendiversary. Because of the way we met, we know the exact date we met, and every year when that day rolls around, we use that as an opportunity to let each

other know how thankful we are to have her in our lives.

- Devotions - Leilani and I do quite a few devotions together. Some are friendship based and some are not. I love the new things I can learn and take away each time we discuss a devotion.
- Hobby Sesh - We are both pretty avid crafters so a good time for us is breaking out the glue guns and paintbrushes and making pretty things. But, you do you. Do whatever hobby it is that you and your best friend may share from aerobics to paintball to retail therapy.

Face to face time and phone calls with my BFF often leave me feeling refreshed, lighter, and happier. It's an important part of my mental health and much cheaper and more convenient than therapy. And honestly, it doesn't matter what we are doing, it's the moments spent together and memories created that are treasured.

<u>Thoughts to Think on:</u>

❖ What is a favorite memory spending time
with your BFF?

❖ What are some ways you can spend time
with your BFF in the future?

"BFFs who pray together, stay together."

Twenty

I'm Calling Your Dad

"In my trouble, I cried to the Lord, and he answered me."
- Psalm 120:1(AMP)

Sometimes you just don't have all the right words to say, and nor could you, in all situations. Some things call for more comfort, wisdom, and knowledge from someone else, someone who knows you better than anyone else; simply put "you need Dad." When I say Dad here, I mean your Heavenly Father because, let's face it, He knows you better than anyone. It may take a strong friend to stop you in your tracks and say pause, wait, hold up - we need to call our Dad on this one.

We kept a list of prayers and praises when these calls to Dad were made. Sadly, what I didn't do is keep those lists in the same place all the time. They were just little notes written in some notebooks or on random pieces of paper. Looking back, I do wish that they all would have been in one place so that I can easily review them, but I know they're there and I've seen many of the prayers filled in with the answers of God's goodness. As I'm writing this, I'm thinking about the fact that we keep a list in the first place. I don't know if it's just us women who tend to be list-makers, but I do know all my women pals do so.

We sure know how to rock a list - all kinds of lists like a grocery list, chores list, baby name list, top schools list, places we're going to live, to-do list and the good old classic pros and cons list. And as for my personal favorite list, that would be the one that brought me to the best husband in the world, the desires of a spouse list. And a little insider information here - Nicole's favorite list is a gratitude list. I hope I named some of your favorites here.

I suppose making a list just came naturally to us for these conversations with Dad. This list has brought more joy than pain because looking back we've seen God work in amazing and mysterious ways. We've looked back on prayers from years past we thought had never been answered, only to find that they had come full circle. Typically, never the way we saw it happening but yet seeing God's plan and reality was better than we could have ever imagined possible. We've stopped ourselves from hours of worry and fear because one of us simply said, "I'm calling Dad on this one." And before we knew it, peace and joy would overcome our hearts and minds in no time. When you are in a storm and you know the one person to help you out may mean you need to eat a fat piece of humble pie. It can be hard to call that person and hard to look at anyone, including ourselves and hear, I told you so, or worse yet, "You knew better." So, we tuck and run. This has been the case in families for centuries- that we think whatever we've done is so bad we can't go home.

Well, praise God we both know the love of our Savior (Dad). It never fails, if I've done anything and feel like hiding from God, anger, pride, worry, or fear has me feeling lost. I can trust Nicole will surely call my Dad on me. Not only will she call my Dad on me, before long we meet together with our Father. A best friend has the guts to help you get back in the right standing and out of hiding. I vividly remember some late night, half-asleep prayers walking through hospital halls together worrying about those what-if moments. Yet, we tightly held on to God's promises. I remember when the doctors did not have any answers or the outcome looked bleak when friends and family even hung on to the worst possible outcomes. Times we had to run off to our Dad together. God does not require flowery words or long-winded prayers. I can safely say some of my favorite prayers have been a simple, "help" and "thank you." Nicole has been my words to God when my heart was so heavy and deep with pain that it was drowning out my own voice. I felt like I was sinking, but there she was, my firm anchor to Christ (and vice-versa) she says of me. More than just mere best friends, Nicole has been a prayer partner and Bible study buddy. She has my Dad on speed dial and if the time comes up and she has to call him for me, well, you better believe she'll do it.

Thoughts to Think on:

❖ What are some circumstances in your friendship when you should have called on God and maybe did not?

❖ What are some instances in your friendship when you did call on God?

❖ How did he answer those prayers?

Act on It:

❖ Start a Praise and Prayer Log with your BFF. (Keep Notes by Google is a great app for this. You can give your BFF access to that note and you can both view, edit it, and check-in.)

"But I can build a powerful fortress for her before she even steps into the day with a prayer for the Lord to protect her heart and give her peace that is completely unexplainable to the world unless you too know the only one who can deliver that kind of peace."

Twenty-One

Price Check on Aisle Five

"For the love of money is a root of all kinds of evil. Some people, eager for money, have wandered from the faith and pierced themselves with many griefs." - 1 Timothy 6:10 (NIV)

Alright, guys, I'm going to talk about the touchy subject of money, so buckle up. Over the years, Nicole and I have seen our finances change a lot, just as our friendship has had highs and lows.

We both know our friendship is based on something much deeper than a dollar amount in a bank account. But the truth is finances always play a part in your life. For instance, we all know that a new dating relationship can be quite expensive. For us girls, it often means new makeup or clothing, dinners, and events. That perfect dress you've been eyeballing in the window for months - you know the one - it's perfect, makes you look slimmer but you've never had a reason to buy it - well, now you do. See how easy it is to spend that money, girls? The same can be true with friendships and sadly many friendships actually end because of finances when you are not careful.

So, don't be shocked when your finances begin to play a part in your friendship. The longer you are friends the more life happens. There are valleys and mountain tops. But when your friendship is based on something deeper than your finances, you'll get so much more out of it.

As mentioned before, Nicole and I live states away so we gather things and collect them over the months. It's fun and rewarding to watch the small trinket collection grow. We are mindful of each other's limits. We are not- and I repeat NOT- buying a friend. Nicole and I have both shared the hard truth of how we have fallen into this trap with other friends from our past. It's easy to find yourself buying friendship; like always inviting someone out to lunch and picking up the tab. Make sure the person is not taking advantage of you and make sure you are not in (as the young ones call it) "fishing for a friend in an empty pond".

Back to those trinkets, well oftentimes they are just tiny mementos from when we thought of each other. Once I bought a ridiculous, hot pink lawn flamingo (one of our many inside jokes) on sale and stuck it in the pile. Fun notepads, pens, books, and socks find their way into this pile. But none of those items mean much to me or have large value but to Nicole their value is immeasurable. How do I know this? Well, because I've been the proud recipient of boxes of sweet, thoughtful, and sometimes fall to the floor laughing trinkets myself, and not only have I been the recipient but so have my children. Nicole has made it a priority to send my whole family the sweetest, most thoughtful gifts. I know the price of some of these items may not be much as they're usually handmade but to my kids, they are the most valuable items of all. Every Christmas season, they pull out an ornament that their "Aunt Coley" has sent them and declare it the most priceless ornament that they have.

If you find yourself rushing at a particular time to the store to buy something just because of a date on a calendar pause and check your friendship. We set guidelines in the past where we were not going to send Christmas or birthday presents. I will add a little disclaimer here after many years of friendship that rule may or may not have been broken a couple of times, but the point is we cared more about our friendship than to stress each other out at already stressful times. The problem is when you care about someone so much you can't help yourself. So, we picked a weird random holiday like Cinco De Mayo or St. Patrick's Day that isn't a costly event and we decided to celebrate then. I never knew getting gifts on Cinco De Mayo could be so fun and full of love.

Have fun with it, pick your own friend's holiday, and decide to celebrate it. Remember if you are expecting a gift, you are not in the right mindset. Nicole has never made me feel obligated to send one thing to her; funny thing is because of that I want to send so much more than my budget could allow and her house could store; so really, it's a win-win. I know she does not want a house full of stuff. It's gotten to where even my husband can go to the store and think, isn't this Nicole? I've gotten countless pictures of items while he is shopping- and, Nicole, you're welcome- I've stopped most of them from ending up at your door. In all seriousness, in the end, it's been little bitty notes that are handwritten or sometimes odd items from a fast conversation that she caught a glimpse of something I wanted - like the time I blurted out, "Aren't tiny, baby post-it notes super useful?" and next thing I know, a giant box of tiny, colorful Post-it's appears in my mailbox. Or, the time I said, "Gosh, I wish I had martial arts stickers for my Happy Planner." I mean, really, who stops what they're doing, writes a note, and sends you little martial arts stickers. Well, my best friend - that's who. And I hope you become that friend now, too. Have fun gifting.

Thoughts to Think on:

* ❖ Ask yourself: is my gift-giving from the heart or because of a day on a calendar?

* ❖ What are some thoughtful but inexpensive gifts you can share with your BFF?

"The beauty in choosing your friends is that they can get to know you for who you are in the moment. "

Twenty-Two
Fight Club

"Therefore put on the full armor of God, so that when the day of evil comes, you may be able to stand your ground, and after you have done everything, to stand."
– Ephesians 6:13(NIV)

Throw the punches and step out of the way. Okay, not really. Fighting doesn't solve anything, girls, especially in our friendships.

Fighting fair seems like an odd term when it comes to friendships or relationships. And honestly, we're not talking about those big knockout, drag-out fights. We are talking about those minor disagreements that pop up in friendships and relationships in the blink of an eye though the same thoughts can apply to those big fights where ya wanna lace up your boxing gloves. To be honest, Nicole and I don't disagree very much anymore. In the beginning of our friendship, we had a few, minor brouhahas but nothing that could not be quickly talked out.

It's important that you have some ground rules in place if you want things to turn out well and put you in a place where you both can move forward.

This is our Friendship Fight Club Five, rules for disagreements that will result in a healthy relationship. Side note: you can use these in any relationship.

1. No low blows, which include name-calling or throwing something from the past in your friend's face.

2. Spell ass-u-me. Don't just assume things. Ask questions and talk it out to know how your friend is feeling.

3. Temperature check. If you're hot-tempered, know that about yourself, tell your friend you need 15 minutes, 20, or even an hour to process your emotions and cool down.

4. You do you, boo. Agree to disagree. It's ok to disagree. Honestly, why are you going to argue with someone that creamy peanut butter is the best when their fave is crunchy. It's a moot point, people.

5. Worldview. Remind yourself what's most important here; I mean, at the end of the day does it really matter if it's blue or if it's purple. Maybe to you, it does so say that. In our friendship, we've always had a scale where we ask ourselves on a scale of 1 to 10 how important this is to us. Really, children are dying in other

countries.

We've had very few disagreements in our friendship, but the one that stands out most is when we were hosting an event together that had lots of little bitty details which meant lots of decisions. One was a fabric choice for an overlay on a table. We could not agree on a fabric. This brings us back to rule number 3 - is it late? Have you both had dinner yet? Have you already made too many decisions for the day and this one can wait till tomorrow? Have these discussions at a good time for each of you.

This is where our Fight Club Rules were born and Rule 5 clearly states we ask how important the silly fabric is to each of us in the first place. For one of us, it was 3 and the other an 8. And just like that - problem solved.

And now many years later, we don't even have to talk about our scale out loud. We just internally ask ourselves how important whatever we are discussing is to us and go from there usually working it out at lightning speed.

Friendship takes a lot of compromises. Working together but realizing you are two different people helps friends appreciate each other more. I think that was the biggest life lesson for us in the fabric debacle- we realized we are different people with different tastes and styles but that's what makes our friendship and collaborations so great. Her strong suits and mine are completely different, but when you combine them with the Fabulous Five list, you have two completely happy friends.

Lastly, always remember girl code when it comes to fighting: hug it out, remove the rose-colored glasses, say you're sorry, move on, and forget about it.

Thoughts to Think on:

❖ Are there any other ground rules you feel need to be added to our list?

❖ Is there something that has happened in a friendship that you have not forgiven your friend for?

Act on It:

❖ Is there something that has happened in a friendship that you need to be forgiven for? Reach out to that friend and ask for forgiveness.

Twenty-Three
Turn Back Time

"For everything there is a season, a time for every activity under heaven." - Ecclesiastes 3:1(NLT)

As we've mentioned before, we do not live in the same state. Some people might find that this makes it tricky to remain close and others might think it makes it awkward when we are finally face to face again. But since we are both suckers for historical women's books and movies, (We love reading Charlotte Brontë and Jane Austen- and Lord, yes, please give us some *Little Women*!) we have taken some cues from their communication styles while adding a modern twist.

One of the things that I find so great about those books and movies that take place in older generations is the simple times and pleasures. Pleasures like writing a letter or in old movies when they get their first phone and the very first person they call is their best friend.

Girl, don't let time or distance be an excuse. Don't let it stop you from keeping that connection going with your BFF. True friendships can withstand the test of time or distance so pick up a pen and send an old-fashioned, "snail mail" letter, pick up the phone and call your best friend, or if you're a risk-taker train a carrier pigeon. Don't wait on them to call you, and don't you dare go into the, "I'm-always-the-one-calling-them" mindset. If you think about them, just pick up the phone or a pen.

Unlike the era *Little Women* is based in, nowadays we have technology to make staying in touch with long-distance friends much easier. There is texting, Facebook, and even a newer app called Marco Polo that is great for on-the-go women who want to send you a message but they don't have time when you have time. You shoot these short vid clips from your home, the pickup line, or- let's be real- the two minutes you have while you're sitting on the toilet. But seriously girls, please just angle that camera up, and no one will be the wiser. It genuinely makes it feel like you are just doing errands or sharing a cup of coffee with your bestie, or going to the bathroom in a pack like all ladies do.

There are lots of ways for you to connect with your best friends. The two of you just have to figure out what works best for you. Generation after generation we've been finding ways to connect. We've had seasons where each of these things listed have been things that we've done from time to time (except neither of us has managed to train a carrier pigeon yet) because as seasons change so do our time frames. And sometimes I have more time than she does and vice versa, but because our friendship is so important to us, we find ways to make it work. The trick is to find the way it works for each individual friendship. And as the saying goes, in order to have a good friend, you've got to be a good friend.

Friendship isn't a 50/50 dynamic. You each have to put in 100 percent. Give it your all; write her a letter, pick up the phone, or send her a video clip. Keeping up regular communication will make it less awkward when you can finally share space in the same room and you'll find yourself picking up right where you left off just as the March sisters did in *Little Women* generations ago.

Thoughts to Think on:

- ❖ What are some ways you can use modern technology to stay in touch with your BFF?

- ❖ What is something you can do right now to let your BFF know that you are thinking about her?

Twenty-Four
Dream a Little Dream

*"Who can tell you what is going to happen. All I say
will come to pass, for I do whatever I wish"*
- Isaiah 46:10 (TLB)

I remember a time I was folding laundry
when my son came in upset and crying after
watching a television show. Once I was able to
calm him down, he explained that the main
character's best friend in the show had died.
After some talking and many tissues, I soon
realized that it wasn't the character he was
mourning, he was mourning the fact that at his
young age he didn't have a ride-or-die best
friend yet.

I started to tell him about my history of
friendships and how when I was his age, I
dreamt and prayed for a friend. I pictured her
in my head; she was perfect, maybe she would
even have some of the same interests and
hobbies as me. I knew that I would have her for
life so from that dream on I was on the hunt to
fill the image in my head. I wanted it so badly
that whenever a new friend popped into my life

with any of the similarities I dreamt of, I was determined to make that person fit in the mold I had created in my head and heart for the perfect friend.

And sure enough, that first friend showed up when I was young. We became close but not really close. Mainly, I pushed myself into a mold so I would fit right into her life, like changing things that are core things about myself. I soon realized I was never meant to fit into that mold. Let me be real with you, I don't like WWE wrestling, nor do I care for video games. Forgive me if you do, judgment free zone here; you do you boo.

Fast forward to my pre-teen years, because those weren't confusing for any of us, right? To make matters even better, I had moved to a new area. Now, remember this is before the days of social media where staying in touch with long-distance friends was easy. Nowadays, you can keep in touch with anyone anywhere in the world with a swipe of your finger. But back then, in case you are one of those who don't know, you basically said goodbye and hoped to stay connected. Staying connected was much more intentional, you had to pay for long-distance, and if you were lucky enough to have a cell phone it was for emergency purposes only. Those friends may be out of sight but definitely not out of mind. Sadly, one lost address or misplaced phone number and it was all over. Now that friend is just a faded memory in the back of my mind.

Let's move into my early twenties, I met someone whom I was certain was going to be my best friend for life. We had so many things in common: young moms with new babies, we were the same age, we lived one street away from each other, and we came from big families. I even taught her nephew in pre-kindergarten for crying out loud. And then there were the simple things: same eye color and complexion - we could even share makeup. She was my height so my closet was hers. We both were seeking a deep connection with a best friend. But a lot of our connections were surface things, some of the deep stuff was still missing. But I was so desperate for a best friend that I refused to see it. I tried to look past the not-so-good things that began to surface in our friendship.

She needed so much help and I needed a project. If you could hire someone to help run your life, that was me. I checked the mail a lot and I never got that paycheck. I helped this girl find a job, a new place to live, childcare - no problem- and even a man! Can we say dating service? I was her swipe right app. I was her full-time nanny, her housekeeper, her employment recruiter, her financial planner, and her therapist. Gosh, just writing all of this makes me feel like I need a raise. Basically, whatever she needed, I did it for her. I was giving, giving, giving, and all she was doing was taking, taking, taking.   In the end, I was tired, burnt out, and I realized that I was never her true friend. I was all of those things above to her. She was none of them to me. The feelings were not reciprocated. I did all of that because I loved her and I felt I was her friend and I was trying to mold her into being mine. I was left broken-hearted. When the truth came out, she wanted my husband more than my friendship. My whole family was left hurt, broken, and in need of therapy due to that toxic friendship. I was left still longing for that best friend I had been dreaming and praying about for many years.

Once I had gotten rid of the toxicity in my life and the clouds were removed, I could see the sun shining so brightly that I saw that God had gently placed someone in my life. That friendship began to blossom and grow. Yes, that friendship is the friend that you're reading about right now. Nicole is there through thick and thin. It's so sweet to know that God had put her there right before that toxic friendship blew up. Nicole has been there to mend my heart and help put the pieces back together. I've never once had to do anything to earn her friendship nor has she. It's been a friendship built on trust and love, give and take, push and pull, and ebb and flow. That's what you are looking for in a friendship. When Nicole came into my life, it was like the storm had settled and I stopped looking for something I didn't have. I realized what I had found was a true friendship. Of course, I can tell you now I didn't know that then, but what I did know is that the peace that surrounded this friendship was very present, unlike any of the others. I never felt like I had to act and entertain as I did in previous friendships. I didn't feel that way then nor do I now. We were just who we were and it was enough. You don't have to fake it till you make it. You do you and find someone who accepts and loves you for that. That's what I found in Nicole.

I said all of that to say that night when I was sharing with my son, I told him, "don't fake it." You'll find that friend, but if you force it instead of letting God make it, you could end up with toxic friendships just like the ones I shared with you. Our God is an all-consuming, loving God and he blessed me beyond measure when he blessed me with Nicole. I pray that same blessing for you.

Thoughts to Think on:

❖ Have you had some friendships in your life that were not godly?

❖ How did these friendships hurt your heart?

❖ Do you have a friendship that is God-centered now?

Act on It:

❖ If you have a God-centered best friend, say a prayer of thanks for her right now. If you do not, say a prayer asking God to send her your way.

Twenty-Five
Say a Little Prayer for You

"But when you pray, go away by yourself, all alone, and shut the door behind you and pray to your Father secretly, and your Father, who knows your secrets, will reward you."
- Matthew 6:6 (TLB)

Do you remember the old sentiment "drop me a line?" Just saying it seems like such an easy task to complete. Well as you probably know by now, it isn't always as easy as it seems. Dropping a line sometimes can be the equivalent of dropping a bomb in the middle of someone's busy day. Come on, ladies, you know the kind of day when the clothes need folding, the kids won't stop screaming, and dinner, if that's even a thing, well, it's late again.

As best friends with Nicole for many years when I see the time on a clock or the dates on the calendar, I know what those mean in her life. I know when graduation dates are coming, birthdays, and even some memorable sad dates. I know what weather changes, early school releases, and holidays will mean to Nicole's little family. Sometimes our hours are long and the days are short, meaning time to be on the phone together isn't always possible. But we can always drop a line via prayer to God. He is always there ready to listen to the concerns of our hearts.

As you know by now, Nicole's son, Noah, has special needs and it often makes her days feel really short and filled to the rim. We can't always be right there with each other, but when I wake up and my clock is flashing 7 AM and I'm able to hit the snooze button 3 more times, I know she is rushing around performing ridiculous antics to get her wheelchair-bound son changed, dressed, and fed before that bus's horn honks. So, then I pause and rollover, and no I didn't hit the snooze button. Instead, I say a little prayer for her. I know what might seem like a normal day to me is not at all going to be normal for her because, in fact, she has taught me that normal is just a setting on a dryer. I know when the calendar rolls around to June 21 or even September 17, she might wake up heavy-hearted. But I can build a powerful fortress for her before she even steps into the day with a prayer for the Lord to protect her heart and give her peace that is completely unexplainable to the world unless you too know the only one who can deliver that kind of peace.

Sometimes, friendship is being a prayer warrior more than a prayer partner. Pray for each other and lift each other up; it's felt more than you'll know. No need to share with them, this is between you and your Heavenly Father. It's not a tool you use to make your friend feel any particular way. With that said, it is also private and not meant for open floor prayer requests. Don't air personal information unless asked to do so.

Perhaps you feel you should pray for your friend but don't know exactly what to pray for. Ask the Heavenly Father to show you what to pray for. Let Him guide you as you begin that prayer.

Make time to pray for the specific needs you know about in your friend's life. You've been given a special privilege into their lives; a front row seat into some of their life's deepest pains and most beloved desires; don't use it carelessly, use it to go to the Lord for them.

Thoughts to Think on:

❖ What are some of the times you felt a strange, unexplainable peace in a hard time?

❖ What are some things or dates you know right off that you could pray about for your friend?

Act on It:

❖ Write down important or hard dates of your BFF 's in your planner and make it a day of prayer for her.

Twenty-six
Battle of the Sexes

"But shall I tell you to act that way, to buy friendship through cheating? Will this ensure your entry into an everlasting home in heaven? No! For unless you are honest in small matters, you won't be in large ones. If you cheat even a little, you won't be honest with greater responsibilities." – Luke 16:9-10 (TLB)

I think there used to be a game show called *Battle of the Sexes,* but that's not what I'm talking about here. No worries, we're still on friendship, but I've got a switch-a-roo for you. Guess what? Not every story is the same, sometimes your best friend might just be someone of the opposite sex. While Nicole has been my best friend for over eighteen years, she doesn't live locally. One of my local besties is a guy. We are really close; my kids even call him Uncle.

So, a little background here, I grew up in a house where I was raised by my Dad with three brothers. I often say that I was raised by what is the equivalent of a pack of wolves because in hindsight I really felt like I was raised by wolves. Now don't get me wrong, it wasn't a bad thing - it was a good thing- so please don't think I'm over here man-hating. Because I'm not. So, go ahead and delete that angry message right now. I felt like I was part of a pack; I had a family that always had my back. I was the only girl in this little family group, and, oddly enough, I'm still the one that loves sports more than the rest of them. There was never much drama around my house, and, honestly, I guess I don't handle it too well today. So, growing up, I found myself hanging out with guys. Everybody always just said, "Oh it's Leilani, she's one of the guys." There were no weird feelings; we all just hung out and had a great time. I love sports, cars, quarter-mile races, and being outside more than inside. I loved climbing trees. When I was little the one thing my Dad would fuss at me for was climbing trees in dresses. He'd ask me to, "Please at least wear shorts." I just didn't think about stuff like that because I felt like I was one of the boys.

If you are in a relationship with somebody else who has friends of the opposite sex, it could be really hard; you may need to set some ground rules. You have to have some boundaries to protect the friendship and to protect the person you are in a relationship with. When I married my husband, I realized most of the people I was closest to, except for Nicole and a few other girlfriends, were guys so that was a discussion we had. I respect my husband and love him. I wanted to make sure that he felt comfortable. I'm sure it's got to feel a little bit awkward when your wife hangs out with other guys, so we set up some boundaries and rules.

I always- and I mean *always*- include him when a guy friend and I go somewhere for lunch, dinner or some exciting fill in the blank activity. You know the one most girls roll their eyes about. Well count me in, I'm there. But I always pause and ask my husband if he wants to join us. This simple act opens up the line of communication so that he knows he's always included.

I'm careful to never badmouth my husband or share our troubles. That's dangerous territory and for another book. A true friend should be rooting for my relationship anyway. We celebrate each other's other relationships. We do things together as groups. Honestly, there's more to me than the mushy stuff. With the guys, we talk about pranks, jokes, sports but also our dreams and goals for life. I dislike TV and Hollywood because it paints all male/female relationships to be romantic. Why can't two people have a great time laughing and carrying on together and not have some relationship that goes beyond the bounds of friendship? I mean, seriously people, you have to respect each other. It is possible to have a friend of the opposite sex and **just** be friends.

Find out what matters to your significant other. Does it mean that somebody's jealous? They could have been hurt before. I love and trust my husband dearly, but sadly I've been hurt in the past. That's not his fault; it is what it is. But because of that and my open honesty with him, I told him how I felt. I wasn't jealous and it had nothing to do with him, it's just that I've got tender scars so if he's going to hang out with somebody, I need complete honesty. Because he knows where I'm coming from, he's careful to make sure that I'm never in pain. He tells me where he is going and who he is going with so it doesn't cause a problem.

That's what love does; you watch out for each other and try not to hit a scar that's already on your heart.

So, no matter how awkward the conversation may be, set boundaries for your friendships with those of the opposite sex and stick to them. And most importantly, enjoy and cherish your friendships whether those friendships are with guys or girls. It's a blessing to have a great friend, so cherish it.

Thoughts to Think on:

❖ Do you have a good friend who is of the opposite sex?

❖ What boundaries or rules have you and your significant other set up to make you both feel comfortable with this friendship?

"She had strength that I did not have."

Twenty-Seven

What Doesn't Kill You Makes You Stronger

"Jesus Wept." - John 11:35 (KJV)

Writing this chapter is the most difficult out of all the chapters in this book, and, honestly, summing it up in one little chapter is just as difficult. It could be another book of its own (Hint, hint, wink, wink). We've been working on this book for years and every time God put this book on the pause, our friendship would go through new territories, tests, and have more stories to tell. Come to find out, this chapter was one of God's pauses.

Have you ever had one of those life-altering days where you know that from this moment on your life will never, ever be the same? Your life will always be divided into two parts- before and after that life-altering event- which makes me think of Christ, BC and AD.

That life-altering, nothing-will-ever-be-the-same day, for me, was September 17, 2019, a normal, warm fall day much like any other day. It was Noah's naptime (you know my sweet kiddo, we've mentioned him quite a few times in this book.) I went through the routine that is Noah's naptime: four pillows, check. A sip of juice, check. Paisley the comfort dog at his feet, check. Three lovely renditions of *Itsy-Bitsy* Spider, check. A promise to call Nana when he woke up, check, another promise to ask about a playdate with Grandad (aka Noah's BFF) check. Finally, I closed the door and let out a little sigh. I love that kid with every ounce of my soul but sometimes he is a tad exhausting. I laid on my bed for a few minutes before making a light lunch for myself, checking email and things on my phone, and doing some quiet housework. When that boy is sleeping, you don't dare wake him up.

I glanced at my watch and realized he had been sleeping for longer than usual, but I just figured he was overtired. The day before was my birthday and he had been up later than his typical bedtime because my parents had been over for a mini celebration. I waited about 10 more minutes and decided to go check on him.

And this is the moment my world came crashing down around me and everything was forever changed...

I went into Noah's room and called him a sleepy head and told him it was time to wake up. I gently shook his shoulder. At this point, I was starting to become concerned. This wasn't like him. He didn't budge. I realized he felt clammy- and it was at that moment my worst fear as a Momma came true- when I realized he wasn't breathing. I yelled for his Dad while frantically running for my cell phone. Hands shaking, I dialed 911 and I fought for my precious boy for 6 long minutes and 58 seconds as I did CPR per the 911 operator's instructions until the paramedics arrived.

And as much as it pains me to write this, the paramedics' words were, "I'm sorry. He's gone." There was nothing they could do to revive my baby. Had you asked me right then and there to write this, these would not have been the words I would have used but with time comes reflection and now I can say that it's comforting that Jesus took him peacefully and pain free in his sleep that afternoon. Sweet Noah was a handful but a heartful. He was a fearless warrior but his little body just gave out. He is free of his wheelchair and can now walk, run, and talk. He can do all the things he couldn't do here on Earth. He is whole. But my heart; oh, my Momma heart... it broke and shattered into a million pieces that afternoon.

That boy loved sleep. He was obsessed with pillows and blankets - he seriously asked for a new pillow as a graduation present. He always wanted people around him to have a blanket and whenever one of our personal care aides left the house for the evening, he'd tell them, to go home and get a blanket and snore. Looking back, it does bring me comfort to know he went peacefully and pain free snuggled in his bed with his graduation pillow, comfort doggie, in his own home safe and sound.

Stunned and shocked, I didn't really know what to do next. The paramedics began asking me a lot of different questions, including what funeral home I wanted to use. As a special needs Momma, I have quite the contact lists. I've advocated, I've got teachers, therapists, doctors - I've got like 18 of them! Pharmacies, poison control, even the local supermarket. But funeral homes? I do not have those on my contact list! But Google came to the rescue in finding a funeral home.

At some point, I knew we had to start making calls and let people know what was going on. Southern etiquette says you have to call your Momma and Daddy first, so that's who got the first call. Tearfully, I shared the news with my Momma that her only grandson had passed away. She said she and Daddy were on their way. I hung up and sat on the floor next to my husband. That was a hard, hard call. Leilani was next. I knew I was going to need my sister to get through what was going to unfold over the next few days.

I don't know if you have ever had to call someone and tell them that a loved one has died but this is not an easy call to make. I didn't know the right words to use so I just blurted out to Leilani that Noah had passed away in his sleep. In hindsight, I should have softened that blow. She responded in typical Leilani fashion with, "No, he didn't." Silly girl, did she really think now was the time for our own *Punk'd* moment! After assuring her this was not a prank, she lost it, which of course meant I lost it again. We consoled each other and I said, "I need you." She said, "I'm coming." It was a very solemn conversation, in which not many words were needed but, in the quietness, so much was said.

I figured she'd arrive the next day. After all, she lives in a different state and it was a little after 3 P.M. But somehow (can we say Jesus, way maker?) my BFF turned into Super Woman and packed a bag within record time, ordered an Uber, and booked a flight while driving to one of the busiest airports in the country. Y'all this girl was there the same evening my son died.

From the moment she and her family arrived, they tagged-teamed duties. I felt so weak. So broken. So exhausted - mentally and physically. She had the strength that I did not have to make phone calls, set up deliveries, talk with the funeral home, looked up scripture, cleaned my house, and so much more. Her husband and kids ran errands, helped rearrange the constant stream of food, and helped usher people around.

I'm a planner by nature but I wasn't prepared to plan a funeral for my 22-year-old son who died suddenly. Leilani was there every step of the way with my husband and my parents as we did the unthinkable of choosing music for the funeral (you better believe *Itsy Bitsy* was on the line up), chose a casket, chose flowers, and made other arrangements that no mother should ever have to make for her child. She was my voice when I was too weak to speak because she knows my heart so well. She held me up - both literally and figuratively. She dressed me - just figuratively - by picking out my clothes.

Her strength in a time in which she too had suffered a loss and was grieving her nephew is what got me through those first few days and more. Even though she had to go home after five days, she wasn't gone. A true friend is always there and strong when we are not.

Thoughts to Think on:

❖ What is a time that your friend was stronger than you were?

❖ How was she there for you?

Act on It:

❖ Thank that friend for her strength.

Twenty-Eight

Girl, I Know How You Feel

"Rejoice with those who rejoice; mourn with those who mourn." -Romans 12:15 (NIV)

"Girl, I know how you feel." I imagine we've all said those words to friends before. I'm guilty of it myself, but the truth is, I don't know how you feel. I don't own your feelings. They're yours. What I do know is the inner depths of my friend's heart because I've known her for so long. You see, the reason I know the depths of her heart is because I have swam through those deep, dark waters with her before. But still, when something bad happens I say the simple phrase that pops in my head time and time again, "Girl, I know how you feel." It rolled right off of my tongue without even a simple thought. That is until my brain and my head collided and I began to think- and I mean, really think- to stop and ponder these simple words. I-know-how-YOU-feel. Then all of a sudden, like a lightning bolt from heaven, those words sounded ridiculous. And as of lately, I've been trying to stop these kinds of phrases from jumping right out of my mouth.

This turnabout was set into motion when the unimaginable happened and our sweet Noah suddenly passed away. I just wanted to be around Nicole and help her chart these new waters. They were stormy, scary, and I felt like she was lost at sea and I had to get there. I wanted to be her anchor, to support her and keep her safe at shore. There were no words that I could say that would make her feel comfortable and at peace and sadly I would blurt out the very phrase, "I know how you feel." Because of my pain at losing my nephew, Noah, I wrongfully assumed that our pain could be equal. But you see my pain is that of an Aunt and hers is that of a Momma. She bore him, loved, nurtured, and cared for him for 22 years. But at the end of the day, I remember thinking I have no idea, no idea at all, the horrible pain she was going through. All I could think is that this loss must be heart-shattering, drop to your knees, world crushing, depths of despair, shipwrecked pain on an unfamiliar island.

But what I've learned is that pain is relative. It's relative to our surroundings and its relative to our life. To one, they could lose a limb and still bounce back and to another a mere papercut could send them to their knees. I'm not calling you a baby or a wuss when you broke your nail last week. What I am saying is that pain is different for all of us. We all process events and life differently. That's the whole reason it's our life. Each of our lives is different; the twists and turns of the things that we've been through, the things we've seen, the family we've had, and the things we've had to encounter. So we don't know what we don't know. We may not understand how our friends feel but what I do know is that God's word says to mourn with those who mourn, not that you have to share their feelings. You could go through the exact same tragedy and completely feel different but you can love, hug, support, console, and show empathy. Or here's one for ya sister, you can even just clean their house.

Choose your words carefully, but for those of you that are hearing the words, that may trigger raw emotion and unpleasant thoughts, you too may want to choose your reaction carefully because it's typically said with good sentiment and with a good heart. So, please put on a filter of love and choose to believe they meant nothing mean or hurtful by their words. And if you still feel like you have to do something, give them your copy of this book with a few highlighted passages (wink, wink). On that day when I said what now feels like dreadful words to Nicole, she chose to look past them blindly because she filtered her reaction with love and she knew that it came from a good place in my heart.

When someone loses someone, you try to relate to them with your greatest pain. I remember when I lost my uncle. A lot of people's reaction was to the tune of, "it's just your uncle." But, let me tell you, losing my uncle was one of the deepest pains. We were very close. Some people don't have that story, maybe they have a creepy uncle and they're not really close to him. But that's not my Uncle - mine was fishing, camping, pies over open fires, singing Little Mermaid Songs on repeat into the wee hours of the night, long card games, and laughing until our sides ached. I'm sorry if yours is not the same story.

We just don't know the depths of other people's relationships, their hearts, or their pain so just be mindful of that. Do not assume and do not judge because you don't know. And, honestly, how could you ever. Just take the time to filter with love your thoughts, words, and actions. It's sure to save you unnecessary pain, keeping you from losing the one person who is always there to bring you back to shore safely.

Thoughts to think on:

❖ What's a time in your life where someone said something that wasn't presented in the best way, but instead of seeing the support in their words, you only focused on how they said it?

❖ When's a time you later realized that you might have put your foot in your mouth? Have you thought to go back and apologize to your friend?

"She was my voice when I was too weak to speak..."

Twenty-Nine

You Deserve All the Gold Stars

"For nothing will be impossible with God."
- Luke 1:37 (NKJV)

If you are a Momma, I'm sure you know all about the days of getting ridiculously excited over small accomplishments when your Little was, well, little. "You went poo-poo in the potty! Who's a big boy? You're a BIG BOY!" Then you proudly hand over new Hot Wheels and a pack of M&Ms as if your child had just played a Mozart symphony or solved the hardest Algebra equation. (Quick side note: my special needs kiddo never went poo-poo in the potty for me. Props to all the Mommas with the walking and talking kiddos out there, I don't know how ya do it. But I do think I deserve an award for changing diapers for 22 long years. Just sayin'.)

Anyways back to the topic at hand: small victories. Even as adults, it's still validating to celebrate the tinier things in life and who better to celebrate them with than your BFF, right? There are points in life where it is just a struggle to be an adult; you know what I'm talking about, girl. Some days it's a major struggle just to get out of bed, get your bra on, or cook dinner without burning it. Those seemingly simple tasks at times may seem momentous and take huge amounts of energy and effort to accomplish. Well, ladies, I have some great news. Recently, I came across adulting planner stickers that celebrated those little things we do each day and bought a set for myself and Leilani. How fun it was to reward ourselves in our planners for those accomplishments that no one really notices! And you better believe, it made it even more fun and meaningful because we were both doing it with the same stickers and could discuss it- and best of all- laugh about our need for stickers at our age. Side note: I blame my kindergarten teacher for this deep-rooted need for stickers.

After my son passed away, I began to battle depression and Post Traumatic Stress Disorder, more commonly known as PTSD. I was surprised that I, an average Momma, would be contending with something like PTSD. I thought this was only something soldiers dealt with. My home became my battleground, and I had to fight every day back then just to function. And, I feel free to confess, at times I still do have to fight this battle of me versus PTSD. Now, I'm not talking just a little high school playground yard fight here, I'm talking full-on, put on your armor because the devil is doing hardcore battle against you. I had gone from being full-time, stay at home, 24/7 caretaker of a special needs kiddo to well, nothing. No special plans to make, no special appointments, no special anything. I felt like the special part of me was gone. I was now just me. And to be completely honest, I had been that all-in, devoted, full-time Mom, and caregiver for so long that I wasn't even sure who I was anymore without those titles. I was struggling big time. I felt like I had no direction and very little to live for. I had such a hectic schedule and an unending to-do list before Jesus carried Noah home. I was a creative planner and even decorated my Happy Planner every Friday like clockwork for the week to come. When Noah went to heaven there were no more appointments, personal care aides to schedule, meds to refill, doctors' appointments to notate - I felt so empty. I honestly wanted to throw my planner away but decorating that planner had become such a creative outlet that Leilani encouraged me just to give it some time.

Slowly, she suggested that I write down three things a day and just focus on those three little things. Sometimes, those three things may have seemed so silly to others. In the beginning of listing three things, they were so basic like taking a shower, getting dressed, or feeding the dog (Paisley the pup is very thankful she made the list - thank you Aunt Lala) but I was grieving the greatest loss of my entire life and I had to take baby steps to get back into life.

She celebrated those tiny victories cheering on this adult woman just for taking a shower and putting on her makeup to look presentable so she could go only to her parents' house to keep her from being isolated in a dark, empty, silent home. This may seem little to you but this took humongous efforts during those days. And slowly the list got longer and before you knew it, I did a load of laundry. I took the dog for a walk and even wandered the aisles of the craft store. Still some days, they went back to just the showers and getting dressed but Leilani was there for every step, every small victory.

You have to start small - you can't let the entire staircase overwhelm you - focus on that first step, and then the next, and then the next, and so on, and let your BFF shower you with gold stars all along the way.

Thoughts to Think On:

❖ What are some tiny victories that you and your BFF have celebrated together?

Act on It:

❖ Send a gold star your BFF's way for a small accomplishment.

"You have to start small - you can't let the entire staircase overwhelm you - focus on that first step, and then the next, and then the next, and so on, and let your BFF shower you with gold stars all along the way."

Thirty
You have Lipstick on Your Teeth

"To do what is right and just is more acceptable to the Lord than sacrifice." - Proverbs 21:3 (KJV)

We all have those times where we have lipstick on our teeth or got our skirt caught in our pantyhose when leaving the bathroom. Well, gosh I hope we all do, or I need more help than I first thought. The point I'm trying to make here is, you need an honest friend to help you be your best self. Sometimes being honest can be difficult, but as I'm sure as we have all heard before, honesty is the best policy.

When you are being honest with your bestie, it's important to keep the following in mind.

1. Give grace with your honesty and your reactions to others. Honesty is the foundation of any good relationship. You can't be a good friend without being honest with your friend. Girl, there have been many times throughout our friendship that I've done something jerky or dumb like accidentally dying my hair pink and

I've been embarrassed to call Leilani and tell her the truth. I'll even small talk and slowly make my way to the subject at hand. And though she is honest and real with her response, she does it tactfully. Giving grace to your BFF when she is being completely honest with you is an important reaction and if the tables are turned and you are being honest with your friend about something, give grace and be tactful with your truth bomb.

2. Agree to disagree. One of my favorite things about my and Leilani's friendship is that I can be brutally honest and, more importantly, real with my thoughts about certain subjects that are often considered taboo to discuss with others like politics and religion. I can say things to her that I've often considered too private to share with anyone else. Ya know, those thoughts that we often think but aren't brave enough to say out loud. She never makes me feel bad for these thoughts. Oftentimes, our thoughts are pretty similar, but if they aren't we agree to disagree. While we are often a dynamic duo, we are still individuals with separate thoughts and feelings and that's OK. Honestly, just love each other through it.

3. Keep your word. This may not seem like it really goes with being honest but it does deserve its own mention here. If you or your friend are often making promises you don't keep, it becomes hard to trust each other and believe that they are going to follow through. But keep in mind, that there will be times when the kids get sick or life just gets too crazy to keep your word. Let the other know as soon as you know you can't follow through. A small acknowledgment goes a long way.

4. Keep it real but loving. A good BFF isn't always going to tell you what you want to hear. But she is going to tell you what you need to hear. When things were getting really tough with my son after he graduated and we could not find a day program for him to attend, Leilani gently and lovingly talked with me about how she thought it was getting time to look for long-term care for Noah. She knew that a lot of those places have waiting lists that are years long and knew I needed to start getting Noah on some lists as we were all growing older and it was becoming more and more difficult to care for him all day, every day. That is not a conversation I wanted to have - no one should

have to think about long-term care for their special needs child, but that is a conversation I needed to have. I needed to hear someone who loved me tell me it was OK to start thinking about those things, to give me a little push in that direction. Never did we know that he would move out on his own and his forwarding address would make Heaven his eternal home.

Real queens fix each other's crowns. Friendship isn't about competition, it's about compassion and companionship which isn't possible without honesty.

Thoughts to Think On:

- ❖ When is a time that your BFF was honest with you about something?

- ❖ How did it make you feel?

Thirty-One

Happily Ever After

"How wonderful it is, how pleasant, for God's people to live together in harmony!" - Psalms 133:1 (GNT)

So we know that "happily ever after" has never been a part of any marriage vows and rightfully so because marriage isn't easy. While we both love our husbands dearly, we are each completely different from them. We argue with them, sometimes disagree, or don't see eye to eye because that's just how marriage works for most people. If you don't have tiffs from time to time in your marriage or relationship with your significant other then we kind of feel sorry for you because that has made each of our marriages stronger.

Strong marriages start with strong vows and commitments. We were in each other's weddings and we witnessed one another say these vows to our spouses. It's almost as if we also vowed to help make each other's marriage work too. They often say it takes a village when raising kids but we also believe it takes a village to make a good marriage. Marriage can be hard work at times and you need a strong friend cheering for your marriage not trying to destroy it. You need someone to vent to during the hard times of marriage, but one thing that can break a marriage is venting to the wrong friend who isn't supportive. Sometimes it can be from a friend who says, "Girl, I know what you mean. I'd leave him." Or perhaps she starts the sentence with "Well, honey what I would do is..." Typically, that's not a good start to any sentence with the wrong motives because what I would do could be beat that man silly with a newspaper. And I don't think anyone needs to start beating folks around here.

But when you have a friendship like ours, you can get good solid advice. You need that ride-or-die person that you can share the deep, ugly stuff with that you don't want anyone else to know. When you are talking with a friend who knows your marriage, she can respond with "you know how much he loves you" or ask "did you eat before you said that to him" and help you put things in perspective. Sometimes that's all it takes to solve a disagreement- a third party to help you see things differently.

Our husbands are both supportive of our friendship, often asking how the other is doing. They get along great and are even happy for all of us to do things together when time allows. Although our husbands aren't at all similar, we think they click because we click and they know how important our friendship is to each of us.

We have always wanted to spend New Year's Eve together with our husbands but it just never worked out until New Year's Eve 2019. The Peach Drop in Atlanta was canceled as well as many other festivities in the South and we found ourselves at none other than the Possum Drop (Alright, calm down. Before you call PETA, no live possums were harmed during the event) in a tiny little blip (seriously, if you blink, you'll miss it) of a town in Georgia. We had a great time together donning 2020 glasses and cheesy New Year's tiaras and saying bye to the troubles and worries of 2019 and hello to 2020. Looking back now, we had no idea what 2020 would have in store for us all as a world.

As ridiculous as this dream of ours was, our husbands are happy that we have each other and they gladly joined in on our little New

Year's Eve adventure. And although they may not admit this to you, they did admit to us that they even enjoyed themselves maybe just a little bit.

Let's be honest, my husband doesn't want to hear about my period cramps, let alone some of the high emotions and hard topics I tend to bring up. Don't get me wrong, he will listen but some stuff he needs to ponder a while longer whereas my best friend can jump right in with both feet. Nothing beats the chatter of my girl pals. Am I right, sisters? It's really great that we have each other as a support system. Having a best friend means you've got someone to cheer you on and dry your tears while having your best interests at heart.

Cheers to you, friends!

Thoughts to Think on:

❖ Is your BFF supportive of your marriage or relationship?

❖ Are you supportive of hers?

❖ In what ways can you support each other's relationships?

Dear Accomplished Reader,

Wow, you made it through twenty years of friendship in thirty-one days. Give yourself a pat on the back. You're now at the end of *Friendship Defined*. We hope you have enjoyed this book as much as we enjoyed writing it. We pray that it brought you and your friends closer together just as it did when we wrote it. Remember, reading it twice is OK, too. Or if you're really adventurous, get the Audible version, and listen to us read you this book. We'd love to hear how our book has made a difference in your friendship(s). Write to us at friendshipdefined101@gmail.com or find us on Instagram @friendshipdefined to stay in touch with us. We'd love to share our story more with you. If you want to invite us to come and speak, we are always willing to see if we can squeeze you in our schedules.

Love,
Your New Month-Long Friend
(Insert our friendiversary date here _____)

Leilani & Nicole

Scripture References

Opening: "May the God of hope fill you with all joy and peace as you trust in Him so that you may overflow with hope by the power of the Holy Spirit."-Romans 15:13 (NIV)

1. "Two are better than one, because they have a good return for their labor: If either of them falls down, one can help the other up. But pity anyone who falls and has no one to help them up." – Ecclesiastes 4: 9-11 (NIV)

2. You have turned on my light! The Lord my God has made my darkness turn to light -Psalm 18:28 (TLB)

3. "A friend loves at all times, and a brother is born for adversity." - Proverbs 17:17 (KJV)

4. "Whoever walks with the wise becomes wise, but the companion of fools will suffer harm." -Proverbs 13:20 (ESV)

5. "Greater love has no one than this, that someone lay down his life for his friends. You are my friends if you do what I command you. No longer do I call you servants, for the servant does not know what his master is doing; but I have called you friends, for all that I have heard from my Father I have made known to you."– John 15: 13-15 (ESV)

6." Friends can destroy one another, but a loving friend can stick closer than family." -Proverbs 18:24 (God's Word)
7. "A cheerful heart is good medicine, but a broken spirit saps a person's strength." - Proverbs 17:22 (NLT)

8. "Weeping may endure for a night, but JOY comes in the morning." – Psalm 30:5 (KJV)

9. "Above all else guard your heart, for everything you do flows from it." – Proverbs 4:23 (NIV)

10. "Lord create in me a clean heart."- Psalms 51:10(TLB)

11. "Listen to good advice if you want to live well."
- Proverbs 15:31 (MSG)

12. "But Ruth replied, "Don't ask me to leave you and turn back. Wherever you go, I will go; wherever you live, I will live. Your people will be my people, and your God will be my God. 17 Wherever you die, I will die, and there I will be buried. May the LORD punish me severely if I allow anything but death to separate us!" - Ruth 1:16-17 (NLT)

13. "And don't forget to do good and to share with those in need. These are the sacrifices that please God."
-Hebrews 13:16 (NLT)

14. "Therefore confess your sins to each other and pray for each other so that you may be healed. The prayer of a righteous person is powerful and effective."
- James 5:16 (NIV)

15. "At the right time, I, the Lord, will make it happen." - Isaiah 60:22b (NLT)

16. "Kind words are like honey—
sweet to the soul and healthy for the body. – Proverbs 16:24 (NLT)

17. "Some people make cutting remarks, but the words of the wise bring healing." - Proverbs 12:18 (NLT)

18. "Just as a body, though one, has many parts, but all its many parts form one body, so it is with Christ. For we were all baptized by one Spirit so as to form one body—whether Jews or Gentiles, slave or free—and we were all given the one Spirit to drink. Even so the body is not made up of one part but of many."-1 Corinthians 12:12-14(NIV)

19. "Teach us to number our days, that we may gain a heart of wisdom."- Psalms 90:12(NIV)

20. "In my trouble, I cried to the Lord, and he answered me." - Psalm 120:1 (AMP)

21. "For the love of money is a root of all kinds of evil. Some people, eager for money, have wandered from the faith and pierced themselves with many griefs."
- 1 Timothy 6:10 (NIV)

22. "Therefore put on the full armor of God, so that when the day of evil comes, you may be able to stand your ground, and after you have done everything, to stand."
- Ephesians 6:13 (NIV)

23."*For everything there is a season, a time for every activity under heaven.*" - *Ecclesiastes 3:1(NLT)*

24. "Who can tell you what is going to happen. All I say will come to pass, for I do whatever I wish." - Isaiah 46:10 (TLB)

25. "But when you pray, go away by yourself, all alone, and shut the door behind you and pray to your Father secretly, and your Father, who knows your secrets, will reward you." -Matthew 6:6 (TLB)

26. "But shall I tell you to act that way, to buy friendship through cheating? Will this ensure your entry into an eerlasting home in heaven? No! For unless you are honest in small matters, you won't be in large ones. If you cheat even a little, you won't be honest with greater responsibilities." – Luke 16:9-10 (TLB)

27. "Jesus Wept" -John 11:35 (KJV)

28."Rejoice with those who rejoice; mourn with those who mourn." - Romans 12:15 (NIV)

29."For nothing will be impossible with God." - Luke 1:37 (NKJV)

30. "To do what is right and just is more acceptable to the Lord than sacrifice." - Proverbs 21:3 (KJV)

31. "How wonderful it is, how pleasant, for God's people to live together in harmony!" - Psalms 133:1 (GNT)

Scripture Copyright Notices

Sources

Holy Bible
www.bible.com

Bible Gateway
www.biblegateway.com

Merriam Webster Dictionary
www.merriam-webster.com

Urban Dictionary
www.urbandictionary.com

Acknowledgments

OUR BIG SHOUT OUT

To the editors Amanda Price, Destiny Kroeber, Kelly Faver, & Michelle Thorne for taking the time to read the first drafts of our mess and helping turn it into this masterpiece & Annalee Neely for pushing yourself out of your comfort level and dreaming up this beautiful cover.

Leilani & Nicole want to thank Bethany for jumping into our already long friendship as if you always belonged.

Nicole would like to give a special thanks to Holly for welcoming her into her new family and becoming more than a niece & to her Momma Anne Lambert for being her first girlfriend and for teaching her the value of Sweet Tea & Jesus.

Leilani would like to give a special thanks to Tracy, Katherine, & Michelle for being the kind of friends you can always pick up just where you left off & Pat Wood and Diana Keheley for the beautiful example of 40 years of friendship for us to glean from.

May God bless each of you abundantly for your gracious gifts to us.

We would never be able to fit all the names of all the ones who helped us along the way, you know who you are and so, from the bottom of our hearts…

THANK YOU!

Thank you
for reading our book.

Let's stay connected

Visit us at:
www.knowknowbooks.com

&

Email us at:
friendshipdefined101@gmail.com

Made in the USA
Las Vegas, NV
22 September 2021